Preface

IN the discussion of the subject it was thought best, as most conducive to a clear and deep impression, to focus attention mainly on some one individual place-name. Much of what is said about it will be found to apply, with quite equal force, to hundreds and hundreds of others.

The field, indeed, presents a wide area for investigation. Students of Gaelic literature—those acquainted with the ancient Irish Epic Tale, *Táin Bó Cúalnge*,[1] in particular, in which the process of name-giving in numberless instances takes place before their eyes, or with the topographical tract in Middle Irish, the *Dinnsenchus*, even in any of its many translations—will be prepared to endorse the statement that there is hardly a Keltic place-name, out of our hundreds of thousands, but was at the outset carefully and intelligently chosen, that is not most appropriate and generally very picturesque in significance. There are no blank titles.

---

[1] = *The Cualnge Cattle-Raid*, done into English by Joseph Dunn, Professor at the Catholic University, Washington (London, Nutt, 1914). The opening sentences of the learned translator's Preface must be quoted, *apropos* though they be of nothing at all:—

"The Gaelic literature of Ireland is vast in extent and rich in quality. The unedited manuscript materials, if published, would occupy several hundred large volumes. Of this mass only a small portion has as yet been explored by scholars."

About the year 1906 the distinguished Frenchman, M. d'Arbois de Jubainville, lecturing at the Sorbonne on the same Irish Epic, was much more emphatic.

"I am prepared [he said] to stake the reputation of the Chair I have the honour to fill in the University of Paris that I can prove that in spite of the ravages of time, and for over 700 years the hostile efforts of a foreign government to destroy it, there yet remains of Gaelic literature a mass as great as that of either Greece or Rome, their equal in literary merit, and far superior to them both in morality."

This, on the authority of a gentleman who was present, Mr. V. Collins, now a distinguished Professor. It can be corroborated by the testimony of another Irishman who also attended the lectures. Most likely, too, the quotation may be seen in the *Revue Celtique*, or in the lecturer's *Cours de la Littérature Celtique*.

Impossible, of course, to examine all of them. Without the adoption of some such device as that above indicated even the small portion of the area to be traversed might easily become both wearisome and bewildering.

It has to be acknowledged that, throughout, names of ecclesiastical origin are first favourites. It may, indeed, be objected that the religious element is brought into exaggerated prominence. This, too, is not denied. It was under any circumstance inevitable. The writer took up what interested himself. No doubt, if a soldier surveyed the same ground, his attention would be enlisted rather by the military or battle terms. And if a poet went over it, his sympathies would be excited by quite others ; and he would prefer dealing with the countless appellations, beautiful in sound and beautiful in idea, that once gemmed Keltic topographical nomenclature ; but which, alas ! cast before the gross and unappreciative have got badly mauled and trampled upon, if not utterly ruined. He, too, would be sure to plead earnestly for a restoration of the originals.

But, moreover, the present writer was constrained to dwell overmuch on the religious aspect. His freedom of choice was restricted by his main aim and object. This was to adduce some little corroborative evidence, third rate in its importance though it be, to justify our right and title to the grand old designation, Island of Saints. It is amongst the last of our possessions ; and even in those days, at this late hour, it is being sought to be snatched from us and appropriated to itself by the nation that robbed us of everything else. Had they the least spark of humour, or sense of the incongruous, they would, instead, repudiate it.

In any case there are few Irishmen, it is to be hoped, who would not set a higher value on an essay for its being mosaiced here and there by a little of both the love of God and love of country. The tastes of others have not been here consulted or catered for. Their appreciation is neither sought nor expected. Their praise or blame is of no account. As a classicist might be prompted to add : What is Hecuba to us, or we to Hecuba ?

DYSERT-DIARMADA; OR IRISH PLACE-NAMES

Dysert-Diarmada

or

Irish Place-Names

Their Beauty & Their Degradation

"Be thine the genial task of making the world,
if not better, at least a little more pleasant
to live in."
—James Payn

"Sing to me the history of my country,
It is sweet to my soul to hear it."
—A Dalcassian to MacLonáin, an
Irish Poet of the ninth century.

BY AN
Irish C.C.

(Permissu Episcopi)

HERITAGE BOOKS
2019

HERITAGE BOOKS
AN IMPRINT OF HERITAGE BOOKS, INC.

Books, CDs, and more—Worldwide

For our listing of thousands of titles see our website
at
www.HeritageBooks.com

A Facsimile Reprint
Published 2019 by
HERITAGE BOOKS, INC.
Publishing Division
5810 Ruatan Street
Berwyn Heights, Md. 20740

Originally Printed and Bound in Ireland:
M. H. Gill and Son, Ltd.
50 Upper O'Connell Street
Dublin
1919

— Publisher's Notice —
In reprints such as this, it is often not possible to remove blemishes from the original. We feel the contents of this book warrant its reissue despite these blemishes and hope you will agree and read it with pleasure.

International Standard Book Numbers
Paperbound: 978-0-7884-2586-8
Clothbound: 978-0-7884-9074-3

PREFACE

A candid friend, whose opinion on the book was requested, replied : " Well, fair enough, considering. But it has one great fault : I don't know when you are serious."

To this I indignantly replied : " Why, every word of it is serious, downright serious ; let the style be grave or gay, or as it will."

" *Ridentem dicere verum, quid vetat ?* " I echoed ; and I followed it up by a second fine quotation from old Horace : *Omne tulit punctum, qui miscuit utile dulci.*

" You remember poor Brother Basil, don't you ? " I continued. " Wasn't he as good a teacher as ever you met ? And do you remember, when he had to talk about, for instance, a helmet's visor, or a castle's portcullis ? He did not take it for granted that we, young fellows, knew the world and all, and slate us if we didn't. He went quietly and took an old helmet out of his little museum—Noah's Ark, you recollect, we used to call it— or a picture off the wall, and showed us what exactly a visor or a portcullis was. And did you notice how he used to make a point of illustrating a subject's driest details by a story of some sort ? And he was right. This was twenty golden years ago. But during all the years since our St. John's Seminary days, amidst the bustle of camp and agora, the story and its lesson remains with us ; the dry doctrine would have been forgotten long ago. Now I have only made an attempt to imitate the excellent Marist Brother ; a feeble attempt, I am sorry to say, but my best."

Horace shook him—he has a great respect for Horace. But he was not convinced.

So I think it but right and fair to forewarn the reader.

Another friend, a Professor of English Literature no less, who also had a read of the manuscript, proved a much more severe critic. Thank goodness, I discovered when all was over that, quite after the fashion of expert newspaper Reviewers, he had barely dipped into it here and there. Shakespeare and Dante and Milton are all that he cares about. And they hardly please him. It is said he has four copy-books chock full of notes on their slips and flaws, in grammar and everything else. I made a great mistake, I confess, to let him have the loan of it at all.

"I have never been able to understand," he began, and he beaming all benevolence, mind you, "why in the world such books are published, good or bad. In honesty they should be set down not as new but as second-hand. Why, there's not a fact or fancy of any worth in the whole blessed thing but is cribbed from Joyce, or your Antiquity Journals, or your old moth-eathen tomes that you think so much about you wouldn't lend one to a Bishop. That's a nice piece, by the way, right enough, about Bishop's Island that you managed to lug in—I must get the lend of the Magazine it's in from you when I'm going—and there are several nice paragraphs from Protestant ministers. They are never done rushing into print, those fellows. But so well they may. Their style is not Latinized and corrupted. They write good idiomatic English anyway, not all as one as other hoity-toities not a hundred miles from me, who couldn't speak plain if they got a fortune, and wouldn't if they could. Polysyllables, polysyllables, nothing but polysyllables for them. Grand, of course, to look at like themselves, but nothing in them." He kept eyeing me as he spoke. I was looking glumly into the fire, cudgelling my brains all the time to make out how I had offended him, and for the life of me I couldn't.

"Of course," he ravelled on, and he beaming still, delighted, as always, to hear himself talking. "Of course," he resumed, "Tom Moore long ago advised people who have nothing to say, but still are afflicted with this *cacoëthes scribendi*—and it is harder to cure than the influenza, I can tell you that—

"'The best of all ways
To lengthen your lays,
Is to steal a few thoughts from the French, My Dear.'

"You know the verses, don't you? But your only good

PREFACE

passages—you will pardon the freedom of an old friend——"
And here he came over and patted me on the shoulder.
(" Aye, cut me head, and give me a plaster," I was muttering
under my breath)—" are openly filched, openly, I say, and
no disguising of it or translating, from Emily Lawless, and—
eh, and—eh, others. It is a mistake young writers make.
For it is just like taking and pitching gold among copper coins,
or champagne into buttermilk. It spoils the whole thing. I
have made it a rule meself never to tolerate anything like
that in my *Belles-Lettres* Class. So signs on it. My boys
have their exercises all of a piece. No *purpurei panni*, I
can assure you, blazoning on their own home-spun tweed,
metaphorically speaking, or their rough corduroy, showing
it up and shaming it. It will be all good broadcloth stuff
they'll turn out, I promise you, when they are a while
under me. Unity, unity, my dear fellow, is Rhetoric's first
and last rule ; and the rule all the time."

" When I write something meself," he began again when he
had taken breath, " please goodness it will be something new
and original. I won't claim as my own a sackful of pickings
and pilferings from a hundred books. Burn it, burn it, for any
sakes take and burn it," he concluded at last. " They might
think you were not at yourself, and that wouldn't suit. You
can do better than that, surely ? So take a friend's advice and
burn it."

When I came to (my precious MS. thrust under the cushion
I was sitting on—for fear), I showed no anger or resentment.
This is entirely to the credit of all the lives of mild and gentle
old Keltic Saints I have been reading up lately. Lucky enough
it is seven years since I opened St. Patrick or the first chapters
of St. Francis de Sales. But with this Fadladeen—by the way,
he has written nothing yet, and I believe never will. On his
own principles he never can—I started a long and acrimonious
enough debate. It would weary you to get over it. It ended,
as arguments usually do, in each holding his own opinion more
stoutly than ever.

When he went out, my Magazine under his arm without saying "by your leave"—I'll never see sight or light of it again—I began thinking. "Well," said I to myself, "there is something or other stinging him, it must be, this evening after dinner. Else he couldn't be so crotchety. He is a good fellow, I won't deny, and means well, but he is sometimes like that."

But let the reader judge between us. For my part I have the persuasion ever since, deep down in my breast it is and no man can pluck it out, that the critical acumen of Professors of *Belles-Lettres* is not up to much. Themselves and their rules and their "new and original" compositions!

I did not, you may be sure, give him the satisfaction of acknowledging that radically he might be quite right. Books "just out," numberless almost as disbanded khaki soldiers, are every year being paraded before us (comparatively very few, though, on Irish matters). Now if it can be maintained that a new book justifies its existence simply and solely by bringing to light fresh facts, or by enlarging the bounds of human knowledge, this one has a poor *raison d'être*. It makes no such claim. Such grand volumes, it is a consolation to think, are, at all events, few and far between; and if they be scientific, the theories of even the best of them run a good chance of being scrapped within a few years of publication.

By an accident, in preparing a lecture for a local Temperance Society, the writer became very interested in the subject. Necessarily depending on an ordinary country library, the wreck of one at that, research, indispensable to the production of a book of the kind just mentioned, was out of the question. The best standard works, however, were consulted. Their statements were almost invariably accepted. They are faithfully quoted and will appear, it is hoped, duly acknowledged. For books not professing to be for reference, nor putting up to deep learning or Socratic wisdom, these, as authorities, seem fair enough. Neither is there felt any very stringent obligation to confine

PREFACE

oneself to a mapped-out field. Down in these parts when a man buys a little farm, should a bog, or a brake, or a bit of sheltering wood, be found included in his purchase, he is not wont to object.

The writing of it was a pleasure, and has been carried on as a pastime. This circumstance may indeed have too highly coloured the narrative in patches, and, should the morose be the judges, especially one whole chapter (Chapter VIII); and so supplied some grounds for candid friend's stricture. All the same, its object was never lost sight of; nor, so far as the writer is aware, does it contain a single fact or assertion, however lightly put, that would shun the most rigorous scrutiny. Convinced, as he is, that it will deepen the reader's love of his own particular district, and somewhat also his love of his old religion and of his ancient country, he has deemed it right, never minding critics, to publish it. If it does not do that it fails on its mission. If it effects it, any other result or consequence is not worth talking about.

He is not without hopes, besides, that its perusal will not be considered too irksome, or come to be regarded as taskwork; but that, while obtaining from its pages some out-of-the-way information on a glorious past and a *stimulus* for acquiring more, the reading of it will give the reader perhaps a little of the amusement that the writing of it afforded the putative author.

Of course, the book is rather long and *humanum est errare*. This old saw, as to its terms, was long ago taught us by those mighty demi-gods, our Classical Professors; though few of us can recall that its embodied wisdom in the slightest degree tempered the acidity of their critical observations. The reader, we trust, will be more generous. The subject is indeed a beautiful one, but many a good case is spoiled by wretched pleading. No matter what care has been taken in weeding them out, it would be presumptuous to imagine that there are no mistakes; and that every statement will pass muster, and be considered faultless and flawless. But, to borrow the sincere words of the humble monk, who will be introduced to you towards the end of Chapter VI, " If I tell it wrongly, or if in the telling I make any error, or omit anything I ought to tell, I pray that it may be forgiven me, and imputed to my ignorance rather than to any malice or desire to deceive."

Contents

	PAGE
PREFACE	v

CHAPTER I
INTRODUCTION 1

CHAPTER II
COUNTY KILDARE 2

  Its Clans—Outlines, a Head—Castles—Round Towers—Monasteries and Convents—Their Confiscation—The Courtmacsherry Carpenter—Its Royal Seats—Foillen's Fate—Mullaghmast—The Fianna.

CHAPTER III
DYSERT 13

  Dysert, What it Means—Common in Irish Topography—Dysert-Nuadhan in Roscommon—Forgotten Kildare Shrines—Moone, the Place and the Word—Parish Naming—The Great Father Pat and his Innovations.

CHAPTER IV
DYSERTS, WHAT THEY WERE 27

  Croagh Patrick and Slieve Donard—Modern Mount Melleray—Mungret or Mungaret?—Kingsley's "Hermits" and Baring-Gould's "Lives of the Saints."

CHAPTER V
THE LAKE DYSERT 34

  Devenish as an Example—Stone Churches and LL.D. "Antiquarians."

CHAPTER VI

THE OCEAN DYSERT 42

Skellig Michael—Modern Caldey—Old World Museums—Ardoilen—Bishop's Island.

CHAPTER VII

FADED MEMORIES 54

Should Local Saints be Forgotten ?—Should Irish Missionary Saints ?—St. Gall—Story—Poem—Note of Apology.

CHAPTER VIII

THE IRISH LAY BROTHER 66

Keltic Saints Ignored at Baptism—High-Sounding Christian(?) Names Substituted—Pictures of Irish Saints Unobtainable—Egypto-Irish Religious.

CHAPTER IX

TOWNS CRADLED IN HERMITS' CELLS 77

Origin of the Name Castledermot—Origin of Dysert-Diarmada, Name and Place—Similar Origin of Kildare, Name and Place—Of Roscommon—Roscrea—Monasterevin and Abbeyleix—Athy—Cloyne—Cork—Fort Augustus in Our Own Days.

CHAPTER X

A DUEL BETWEEN NAMES 89

Dysert-Diarmada or Castledermot, Which Wins ?—The First Scores on Sound and on Derivation.

CHAPTER XI

DYSERT-DIARMADA WINS AS A PLACE-NAME . . . 93

CHAPTER XII

AN OBJECTION FROM SHAKESPEARE 98

CONTENTS

CHAPTER XIII

Irish Place-Names Disfigured 100

Slievenamon and Dromahair—Loop Head—Mutton Island—The Twelve Pins—The Ovens—Sion Hill—Leix—The Calf Islands—A Royal Proclamation—Meaningless Jargon—Highland Names—An Indignant Correspondent—Buried Labours.

CHAPTER XIV

Ireland as a National Art Gallery . . . 107

Battles—Portraits—Groups—Legends—Sports—Historical Events—Penal Scenes—Landscapes.

CHAPTER XV

Dysert-Diarmada as a Painting 119

Recalls a Glorious Past—A Key to a Gallery of Local Pictures—A Verbal Shrine—Illustration—The Sin of Castledermot—Conclusion.

CHAPTER XVI

A Ready-Made History of Dysert-Diarmada . . 125

Local Writers—The Sacred Isle and the Sacred Promontory—Camden's Mistake—The Gaelic League—Historyette of Castledermot—Supplementary Facts.

Index of Place-Names Explained 135

General Index 147

Chapter I

INTRODUCTION

CASTLEDERMOT, properly Dysert-Diarmada, is a small town of about 700 inhabitants in County Kildare.

It is a very old town and well worth talking about on its own account.

Its name by itself is worth talking about. It shows up the vicissitudes of Irish place-names; and it illustrates this, too, that much of the glory of the past, suggested by the original name, is obscured and hidden away by barbarous modern un-Irish terms.

It is worth talking about if only for its crosses. But then Miss Stokes in her charming work, " High Crosses of Castledermot and Durrow," has said all that is to be said on that subject. Vallancey, too, an Englishman who posed as an Irish archaeologist, wrote about them *ad nauseam*. Pure unadulterated nonsense it is and in pompous Johnsonese. So you can have your choice in styles, plain English and common sense or bombastic balderdash.

Lastly and mainly it is worth talking about, because the discussion will, it is hoped, bring out this; how full of interest are our little towns if only we would gather up some little of the history and romance in which they figured. As it is, for most of us, it is to be feared, our towns and villages, apart from the ties and glamour of early associations, are just so much stone and mortar, so many marts and warehouses by the river's brim—nothing more.

Chapter II

COUNTY KILDARE

ITS CLANS—OUTLINES, A HEAD—CASTLES—ROUND TOWERS—
MONASTERIES AND CONVENTS—THEIR CONFISCATION—
THE COURTMACSHERRY CARPENTER—ITS ROYAL SEATS
—FOILLEN'S FATE—MULLAGHMAST—THE FIANNA.

" Pillar and architrave
Now fill a common grave,
Tempests around them
Wantonly brawling ;

Stands the old castle still
Crowning the nearest hill,
Angel of death and ill,
Mocking the fallen."

(From poems written, and forgotten as soon as written, by a Maynooth Student.)

CASTLEDERMOT is in County Kildare. This county was erected in 1210 in the reign of King John of England, King John of the Magna Charta. It was one of the first mapped out. It was formed out of three native territories and a large portion of a fourth.[1] The O'Tooles, O'Dempseys, O'Dunnes, O'Connors Faley, and the O'Byrnes (originally called O'Brians) were the main clans inhabiting and owning these territories. Despite wars and confiscations many of them managed to hold on, and these names are once more plentiful in Kildare. Though the O'Byrnes were driven into Wicklow by the Anglo-Normans, they flourished after their expulsion, and some of their descendants returned to the home of their fathers. Another Keltic county family, as we may term it, is the MacKellys. Their chiefs had their stronghold at Rathascull, three miles north-east of Athy. The last master of Rathascull was the remarkable Gicrode-Crone MacKelly. He held it against all comers. When he died, the MacKelly district was divided between the Fitzgeralds, the Fitzhenrys and the Keatings.

---

[1] The Kildare Archaeological Journal, Vol. I. contains an admirable article on these divisions by the late Lord Walter Fitzgerald.

If you look at a good map of County Kildare so formed by King John of the Magna Charta—but not too closely—you will be struck by its resemblance to the head of a man. And it is of a man, too, who carries his head high and proudly.

And well may Kildare carry its head high. It has many things to be proud of. Nor is there a county of the thirty-two which can overmatch it for either historic interest or monuments of the past.

Its Henry VIII castles in the north-west—Kinnefad and Kishavaun, for instance—between the headwaters of the Boyne and Barrow, built to bolt and bar the sole door of the English Pale already shut fast against the Irishry by the Bog of Allen, were not unimpressive, though there is little left of them now. But they are too near our own times. Leland's "History of Ireland" starts with the Norman Invasion. Dr. Johnson, the great English critic and lexicographer, remarks of it :—

"Dr. Leland begins his history too late ; the ages that deserve inquiry are those times, for such there were, when Ireland was the school of the West, the quiet habitation of sanctity and literature." [1]

Besides, like Carbury, Carrick, and Mylerstown castles quite close to them, and indeed like all the castles, they belong to the era of Kildare's eclipse. It would be saddening to think about them.

Its Round Towers are older than these by at least 300 or 400 years. And there are more than half-a-dozen of them; *viz.*, Castledermot, Kilashee, Oughterard, Moone, Old Kilcullen, Taghodoe, one of the earliest type, and Kildare, usually said to be one of the tallest in Ireland. It is 105′ 6″ high; not 136′ 7″, though, as Dr. Healy, copying the authorities before him, has it. Conquerors of time these " gray old pillar temples," [2] they " stand sublime " elsewhere by " the lakes and rushing rivers," here mostly on the plains. A Kildare man must be proud of them. Petrie, too, very exhaustively treats

---

[1] Boswell's Life of Johnson, *anno* 1777.
[2] Temples at least in Schiller's sense :
" Time consecrates,
And things grey with age become religious."

about them, and we would only have to borrow from his pages. But to quote him would be to spoil him; to condense, to ruin the interest in them, and cloud and dim their glory. His the touch of a Master hand, ours the faltering sketch of an admiring pupil. Moreover, in the first volume of the Kildare Archaeological Journal, Lord Walter Fitzgerald gives an exhaustive list and most careful description of Kildare's Round Towers. To it we would refer the reader. But that we have before us the careful measurements of this local antiquary it would be presumption to question the authority of such an historian as Dr. Healy even on such a minor point as the height of one of them.[1]

As to its monuments of piety; an elaborate folio volume, " The Atlas and Cyclopaedia of Ireland," is at our hand. It is published by Murphy & McCarthy, New York, an Irish firm, no doubt, and well turned out. Gorgeously bound in green, with a Round Tower, a harp, and a wolf-dog half the height of the Round Tower, on the front cover, it is manifestly intended to catch the eye of the Irish exile. And it does. Returning, weighty and bulky and all as it is, he would no more leave it behind than he would his " Key of Heaven "; or than a countrywoman going to a Mission would come back without a highly coloured picture from the ' stanin'.' This—the Story of Ireland incorporated with it—an equally gorgeous Lives of the Saints, and Old Moore's Almanac, constitute the Reference Library of many a cottage and little farmer's house; and excellent it is. The Atlas describes succinctly and in vivid, we might say florid, colours Castledermot Abbey, " that splendid relic of Irish ecclesiastical architecture," the home of the Franciscans, " that heroic order that in penal days so unflinchingly braved the sword of persecution." " There are many other abbeys and remains of noted structures in the county of Kildare," the vigorous paragraph concludes, " around which storied memories cling as thickly as the ivy that covers their walls."

---

[1] Inishscattery Round Tower is always given as 120 feet high. A Maynooth student who found his trigonometry all theory (he would not touch a theodolite), measured it for us in a simple way, by comparing the length of its shadow with his own of a summer evening. He is himself six feet and he assures us it is 126 ft.

But it would be sadder still to recall these "storied memories," stories of plundered homes and ruined shrines. Ivy-grown and nettle-covered are the shattered glories of Adare, Kilmallock, Boyle, Sligo, Clonmel, Lisgoole, Creevelea, and of a host of others, no less than those of Great Connel, Kilteel and Castledermot in Kildare, or of Bective, Newtown, Slane, Trim, and Kells in Meath beside it.

"The English after all done a great dale for this country," said a Tipperary jarvey to his English fare as he drove him back to Cashel after visiting the majestic Cistercian ruins of Holy Cross Abbey on the Suir.

"Why, what did they do?" asked the Englishman rather surprised, as the previous conversation was of a different pattern, and no way led up to this eulogium.

"Look at all the fine ruins what they made for the towerists," he explained.

The American "Atlas and Cyclopaedia of Ireland," above referred to, is crowded with such ruins—the most attractive pictures of the old land it had to present to its readers!

For every county is full of them. Except at Multyfarnham, what old monastery is there in the country that is not a ruins? What monks in Ireland have to-day even a corner to shelter them of their ancient noble cloisters? Monte Cassino of St. Benedict and St. Columbanus's Bobbio in Italy are where they were in the fifth or sixth century despite Hun and Vandal. But Mellifont and Asseroe and Kilcullen are in the dust. "Pillar and architrave now fill a common grave." They met with less merciful Huns. The Northern Vandals were the greater Vandals. Thank God the Religious Orders are back with us again, and often, too, near the dear old spot sanctified by their brothers' and predecessors' blood as well as by their prayers. But they must look wistfully across the river or valley at the old foundations. For there,

> "Rite, incense, chant, prayer, Mass have ceased.
> All, all have ceased! Only the whitening bones half sunk
> In the earth now tell that ever here dwelt monk,
> Friar, acolyte or priest."

Nay, without a single exception, what great Irish Catholic church—or small one for that matter provided only they came at it—antedating the nineteenth century is there anywhere in Ireland, that is not a wrecked pile, the home of the owl and the jackdaw ? What one of them was not the victim of thorough-paced English vandalism ? or if not, was unseized upon by the confiscators and is not now in the hands of the confiscators' descendants—as a place of worship(!)—men who, adding insult to injury, rate us and lecture us on our extravagance in church-building, when we try feebly to replace them ? And there were a score and more of magnificent ones—Holy Cross, Sligo ; St. Mary's, Limerick ; St. John's, Longford ; St. Canice's, Kilkenny ; St. Mary's, Cavan, till it was let fall into decay ; St. Mary's, Killaloe ; Qld St. Patrick's, Armagh, etc., etc. But—

> "The hungry, heartless, insane stranger came,
> And never since that time
> Before their torn altars burned the sacred flame,
> Or rose the chant sublime."

A Henry VIII ukase was issued in 1539. It decreed the appropriation or, to be less euphemistic, the wholesale plundering of the monastic property of the Irish Church and the ruthless expulsion of the doomed inmates from their consecrated homes.

In a short time, to quote the historian of the diocese of Meath, Fr. Cogan, nearly six hundred monasteries, fifty cathedrals, and numerous colleges were invaded and gutted, besides sundry places of pilgrimages, hallowed by a thousand recollections and enriched by the pious offerings of successive generations.[1]

We can readily realise the feelings of its Courtmacsherry carpenter when one day, about the beginning of the seventeenth century it was, a band of 150 English soldiers broke into Timoleague Franciscan church, the pride of the splendid monastery, as is always the church, and, amidst the wailing and entreaties of the people, forthwith set about wrecking it to the best of their ability—

---

[1] To add insult to injury, Fr. Cogan continues, the Comissioners of Henry VIII summoned the community of each monastery to go through the mock form of a 'voluntary surrender,' and the religious were obliged to yield to force, in the same way that a traveller surrenders his purse when the blunderbuss of the highwayman leaves him no other alternative—p. 99.

destroying the altars, tearing down the oil-paintings, smashing the beautiful stained glass windows. The poor carpenter was indignant; but it was with St. Francis he was indignant for permitting the sacrilegious havoc. " St. Francis," he broke out, " thou in whose honour this house was built, I know thou art a great friend of God's, and can get whatever thou askest. Now I solemnly swear that I will never do another hand's turn for this monastery of thine if thou dost not speedily wreak vengeance, hot and heavy, on them wretches—not if the Abbot walked on his two blessed knees to me down to Courtmacsherry."

It would appear that his simple prayer was heard. The very next day O'Sullivan Beare met the wreckers and of the 150 but one escaped.[1]

But it is ever thus in any case, explain its happening as you will. If it is not to-day it will be to-morrow. Nemesis in the long run always overtakes the despoiler of church and cloister. A curse seems to cleave to him. " No estates come oftener into the English market than the confiscated heritages of the monasteries," remarked recently an English newspaper. Our Irish experience is just the same. The inference is obvious.

Hundreds of definite instances in past times might be adduced. To select one of them: During the visit of Henry II to Ireland in 1172 a band of Anglo-Norman soldiers who were stationed at Finglas, cut down the grove of yew or ash-trees that sheltered St. Canice's church, Kilkenny. Within a few days, as Giraldus Cambrensis records, they all perished to a man by plague and shipwreck.[2] Yes, the hand of God, if it afflicts and perfects His faithful servants, at the same time protects and avenges them.

In 1539 the Irish Lord Deputy, Lord Leonard Grey, and the Dublin Council tried to save six, only just six, of our Irish religious houses from Henry VIII's rapaciousness. They petitioned him for their exemption from the

---

[1] Meehan's " Irish Franciscan Monasteries," p. 57.
[2] " Social History of Ireland " by Joyce, Vol. I., p. 360.—Another instance is incidentally given later in this chapter (v. p. 10 note) and still another in the last chapter. Dermod MacMurrough died in 1171 of a most loathsome disease, " by the miracle of God," state the Four Masters, " and of Columbkille and Finnian and the other saints of Ireland whose churches he had profaned and burned." The attack of the disease began to be felt soon after his plundering and burning of Clonard, assisted by Strongbow's son and the English. This was the last sacrilege he perpetrated.

order of suppression on the grounds of their indispensable usefulness.

" For," said they, and quaintly it sounds to us, " in these houses commenly and other such like," " all comers are most comenlie loged at the costes of the said houses. Also in them yonge men and childer, both gentlemen childer and others, both man kynd and women kynd, be brought up in vertue, lernyng, etc., etc., to the great charges of said houses," " the woman kynd of the hole Englishrie of this land," in one house and " the man kynd " in the other houses, etc., etc., etc.[1]

Need we add, it was all no use. Great Connell in Kildare, and Kells and Jerpoint in not distant Kilkenny, though among these six religious houses spending themselves in almost incredible hospitality, went with the rest. As ever in Ireland, " the law " had to be obeyed.

It would be disheartening, we repeat, to dwell upon these memories. The more architecturally beautiful were the material buildings and the more refining in their influence, the more generous to the poor and hospitable to the stranger were the inmates and the more spiritual and devoted to the ways of prayer and peace, the more pathetic the tale. They were centres of light and learning. But every thought about them must lead up to the one sickening thought—the thought of their desecration, or of their barbarous destruction and the accompanying sad if glorious martyrdoms.

" Who prayed, who pleaded, spoke in vain,
They struck the babbler to the earth."

But, not to speak of its castles, or its pre-Anglo-Norman Round Towers, or its monasteries and convents; nor, quite another matter, to refer to the scene and associations of the great Isthmian games held in South Kildare, six miles from Athy—commonly called the Fair of Carman, though to us the name suggests but one of the purposes of this

---

[1] Joyce, I., 333. The English religious houses were equally hospitable until this first *Fidei Defensor* " reformed the Church " by the wholesale robbery of its property. Even Dr. Jessop, thorough Protestant as he is, denounces the ring of " miscreants who robbed the monasteries in the reign of Henry VIII, and the ten times worse ring who robbed the poor in the reign of Edward VI." Then came Puritanism to put out what little light was left in their lives, and ' Merrie England," as a commentator observes, ceased to laugh—at least outside an ale-house.

triennial provincial gathering, the most celebrated in Ireland, and that the least important one—[1] Kildare had within its borders many of the residences of the famous old Kings of Leinster. For their day they were palaces.

At Naas (*i.e.*, Nás-Laigen—the assembly-place of Leinster) Leinster rulers lived and held their court till A.D. 904.

In St. Patrick's time Dunlung was the monarch who, as Carew puts it, " swayed the sceptre of Leinster."[2] It must always be borne in mind that in the eyes of those remote ages, when the world's speediest express was the pack-horse, Ireland as to size was somewhat as Europe or great China is in our own days, and Leinster then had an importance quite equal to France's at the present. Paradoxical as it may seem, the world though enlarged has grown very small. As the Saint on reaching Meath made straight for Tara, so on entering Leinster he at once directed his steps to Naas, the seat of government. The two princes, Illand and Alild, were forthwith convinced of the truth of the Gospel; and, what is better, obtained the grace of conversion. But all were not so docile or so blessed. In the royal household there was an old officer, Foillen by name, who hardened his heart. He would listen to no disparagement of his pagan deities. When, out of courtesy to the royal train, he had to, all through St. Patrick's sermon, simple and eloquent and all as it was (we may be sure) he affected to be sunk in a deep sleep. But swift retribution, it is written, overtook him. His sleep glided into the sleep of dreamless death. He never awoke from his pretended slumbers, nor will he till the day of judgment.

Foillen's fate is worth going out of our way to tell about. It ought to be a warning, if anything can, to people who are given to dozing during our long and prosy lectures. It ought also to be a lesson even to those who nod over our improving and highly edifying books, fat with facts, which would do them any amount of good, if only they would keep awake and read them. In that part of the country Foillen's fate was long remembered. The direst curse that

---

[1] Carman was anathematised in the sixth century, for the same causes as in the nineteenth were all our old 'patterns.' Then the Assembly was removed to Naas. The easiest way to cure a kicking horse is to shoot him. But it is a pity sometimes.
[2] " Ecclesiastical History of Ireland," p. 95

an Offally man could invoke on an enemy was the imprecation, " May your sleep be as sound as Foillen's in the Castle of Naas ! "

Naas has two moats and many ruins about it. In the twelfth century it was fortified by the English, and from then ceases to interest us.

Five or six miles east of Athy, overlooking the site of Carman, is the royal rath of Mullaghmast.[1] It is very old and very famous, but since the sixteenth century infamous. For no more diabolical deed blackens the pages of Hunnish or even of Irish-English history than the massacre of Mullaghmast. Four hundred guests invited to a banquet were hacked to death by their host as they in twos and threes joyously entered this fort, unarmed and unsuspicious. The date was 1577. The diplomat who planned, deliberately planned and mercilessly perpetrated, the butchery as a short cut to conquest, the English General, Sir Francis Cosby. And the victims were the flower of the young Irish nobility of Leix and Offaly. As many as one hundred and eighty of the O'Mores and their kinsmen were among them. No wonder there arose a young Rory O'More. Success to him ! He had it.[2]

The Hill of Carbury was once called Side-Nechtain, *i.e.*, Nechtain's Fairy Hill; and again, according to the old documents, Nechtain in the long, long, ago was Leinster's monarch.

On the summit of the round hill of Knockaulin, near Kilcullen, is a royal dun. The area within the huge ramparted wall is thirty-seven statute acres in extent. It is probably the largest fort in Ireland. " Within this spacious

---

[1] Or, but less commended, Mullamast. Older, Mullach-Maistenn—the hill of Maisten. Maistiu was the royal daughter of Aengus (Latin, Aeneas) the Firbolg. She was celebrated as an embroideress. So Joyce. Others translate the name as the " moat of decapitation." *Si non vero, ben trovato.*

[2] A few years afterwards Cosby fell in the English disaster of Glenmalure. A like doom tracked his children from generation to generation. In 1597 at the rout of Stradbally Bridge, in the O'More country, both his son, Alexander, and his grandson, Francis, were slain on the same day by the avenging Rory Oge. It is doubtful if one of the race of this greatly infamous knight remains.
—(" Story of Ireland ")
Rawson in his " Statistical Survey of Kildare " also tells the oft-told tale. " A descendant of the murderers," he states, " never sees his son arrive at 21." " The properties so acquired," he adds, " have melted away and gone into other hands." This is fresh testimony to what was adduced a few pages back (*v. p.* 7), and by a member of the Dublin Society. Success succeeds, but success in evil-doing seldom.

enclosure," states Joyce, " stood the spacious ornamental wooden houses in which, as we learn from our records, the Leinster Kings often resided." [1]

Knockaulin, the ancient Dun Ailenn, overlooks the Curragh of Kildare, and from time beyond the ken of history the Curragh was famed far and wide for the royal sport of horse-racing. It is referred to by the annalists as Curragh of the Races. Punchestown is also in Kildare. It is nearer Dublin by half-a-score miles, but its racecourse in its origin is nearer our own times by perhaps close on two hundred times that number of years. The Curragh is said to be the finest racecourse in the British Isles. Not unlikely it is as fine as there is in the world.

Lastly, on the Hill of Allen, beside Newbridge, was the residence of the famous Finn of the Fianna, though, owing to a *geiss* (prohibition) that was upon him he could never sleep there more than nine nights running. Finn, if he had no crown, is more renowned than any king of them all. Macpherson, to whom our present Chief Secretary is said to be related, in his poems of Ossian tried to transfer him to Scotland under the name of his hero Fingal—the only unsuccessful instance of Scotch pilfering that we know of. There is no rath on the Hill of Allen. The Fianna never raised raths. They did not need them. But on the flat-topped summit, on the spot where once stood what we should now call Finn's palace, a tall pillar tower has been erected. It is a conspicuous object in the landscape. We admire the taste of those who put it up. As a memorial to the full-blooded old Pagan it is as appropriate as is the Keltic limestone cross for a Catholic Irishman. The poet. T. D. McGee, laments that the

> " Fenian heroes now no longer range
> The hills of fame ;
> The very name of Finn and Gall sound strange."

Whatever about the first statement, the second cannot be true, at least in Kildare, where they raised such a memorial.

---

[1] Joyce, II., 94. Those who have seen the Elizabethan wooden houses that still remain and render picturesque the Midland towns of England can form an idea of how beautiful such structures may have been. The most attractive building in the Cathedral City of Hereford is one of them. It adorns the central square and is now used as a bank

DYSERT DIARMADA

To fill up the details of our imagination of Kildare as a man's head, the northern baronies, if the map is tinted, show up as a Glengarry cap; or, as we should prefer to say, an Owen Roe O'Neill foraging cap (for which, if you happen not to know the pattern, see not your town draper's dressed windows, but your " Story of Ireland," p. 367). The cap is braided by the Royal Canal and the Midland Great Western Railway, which run along the top; and the loose braid is studded and starred by Leixlip, Maynooth and some other little towns and stations up to Moyvalley. A school-boy would be sure to notice—and remember—that, of the places mentioned in the preceding pages, the town of Kildare and the Curragh are on the cheek bone; that Kilhill, about six miles east of Naas, is at the back of the head [1] amidst the stray curls of the Wicklow mountains; that Newbridge is about the ear, Athy at the throat, and that on the West Offaly promontory (coloured unfortunately a glowing red in the map before us), which is the nose, a Police Barracks is pendent.

The barony of Kilkea and Moone forms the neck. Centreways, like a rich jewel on an invisible golden torc round the neck, is the little town of Castledermot which we are going to speak about.

---

[1] Appropriately enough, since its commandery for Knights Hospitallers, founded by Maurice Fitzgerald in the thirteenth century, is almost forgotten Equally forgotten is their house at Kilbegs, four miles north-west of the same town

Chapter III

DYSERT

DYSERT—WHAT IT MEANS—COMMON IN IRISH TOPOGRAPHY —DYSERT-NUADHAN IN ROSCOMMON—FORGOTTEN KILDARE SHRINES—MOONE, THE PLACE AND THE WORD— PARISH NAMING—THE GREAT FATHER PAT AND HIS INNOVATIONS.

AS to its name, Castledermot was first known as Dysert-Diarmada. For centuries it was known as that and as nothing else.

Dysert, the first half of the compound, means of course a barren or sequestered district. As a word it is very interesting. It is common to most of the modern European languages. It is spelt practically the same way, and means the same thing, in all of them. This suggests a primitive Aryan origin. More probably both Keltic and Latin have equal claims to it; for out of all the circle of Indo-European languages Keltic comes nearest the language of Horace and Cicero.[1] Otherwise its presence can only be accounted for by saying that it came into Gaelic, as it did into the others, from the Latin; just as it was, sound and sense. That was long and long before its employment here. By then it was completely naturalised, and as Irish as Irish could be.

In Anglo-Irish writings it is found spelt in three or four slightly different ways, *dysert* and *dysart*, *disert* and *desert*. Analogy favours the first. To be consistent we will adhere to it. But there is little to choose between them.

Dysert has also half-a-dozen corrupt or well-worn forms. They are not so easily recognised. *Tristle* is one of these. Hence, thanks to Joyce, we can make out, though it puzzled many, how Dysert-Diarmada could be called *Tristle*dermot in the time of Edward Bruce (1315–1318.) *Tirs, ister, ester,* and even *easter*, are others.

---

[1] " Literary History of Ireland," by Douglas Hyde, p. 11

Dysert is generally used in an ecclesiastical sense, testifies Joyce, to denote a hermitage, such secluded spots as the early Irish saints loved to select for their little dwellings ; and it was afterwards applied to churches erected in those places. The word is of frequent occurrence in Irish place-names. That it is—that like *soggarth* it probably came in St. Patrick's time from the Latin—that as a term it is often well worn and therefore must have been much used, are three facts which, taken one by one, bring respectively clear and unmistakeable corroboration to three distinct things for which we find elsewhere abundant direct evidence ; namely, the number of Irish anchorites in these early times, the Church to which they belonged, and the respect and veneration paid them through the length and breadth of the land. Up and down through the country the word is embodied in perhaps as many as a couple of hundred of our place-names of religious origin.

Dysert often holds well its ground in Irish topography. We have still plain enough *Dysart* O'Dea in Clare, famous, among other things, for its Keltic Cross ; *Dysert*-Aengus in Limerick, and *Dysart*aenus in Queen's County (hermitages of St. Aengus the Culdee who died about 820) ; *Desert*egny parish, *Desert*oghill (—the hermitage of the yew wood) and *Desert*martin, a town and parish (—Martin's hermitage), in Derry ; *Desert*serges, a parish, in Cork (—Saerghus's hermitage) ; and there are some more place-names besides these in which the word cannot be mistaken. *Desert* Chuimin (—St. Cummian's hermitage) in Tipperary changed into Kilcummin parish, not a very violent change. But the parish of *Desert*-Nuadhan in Roscommon (—St. Nuadha's hermitage) has had many ups and downs ; indeed, it may be said as many metamorphoses as a butterfly. It changed into *Isset-* or *Issert*noune, which into *Ester*snow, which naturally into *Easter*snow. Estersnow the old Ordnance maps print it.[1] Easter-Snow the penal Registry of 1705 has it. Eastersnow, hyphenless, the Statistical Survey of the County, published in 1832, designates it in its table of parishes of the Barony of Boyle.

But like a butterfly to the last this, the latest transforma-

---

[1] A Fr. Farrel Berne then "pretended to be Popish Priest" of "Killola and Easter-Snow."

tion of the chrysalis Dysert-Nuadhan, had but a short life. It has disappeared completely from the diocese of Elphin's list of parishes; or else, which is incredible, it has flitted away, fifty miles away, from the north to the sunny south of Roscommon and settled down, easily recognisable once more but draggled a bit, on another Elphin parish near Ballinasloe—Dysart and Tissara. Dysart and Tissara, however, is quite a distinct name. It has its own story to tell, most likely of an old saintly hermit, if only we could come at it.

St. Nuadha's name is gone. Only the very old people, God bless them! are striving to keep it alive by continuing to speak of their ancient parish on the verge of the Plains of Boyle as Tirs-Nuadhan. It is in Eastersnow, which is generally heard, right enough, but well hidden away, and as needy of explanation as the local obelisk. Indeed, seeing the plain significance of the name Eastersnow and how transitory, at least in print, it actually proved, one is tempted to fancy that it had not the least thing to do with St. Nuadha, but was first applied to the parish in a humorous mood by some Tullyboy prophet.

As to the saint himself, friend and fellow-labourer and all as he was of St. Patrick's, he is quite forgotten; his Holy Well, Tobernooan, unfrequented, his cave and home by Loch Uama unknown, his special intercession, of course, never invoked.

Few of the inhabitants of Boyle are aware, writes the local author of "The Antiquities of Boyle," that the names Eastersnow and Cavetown are perpetual memorials of St. Nuadhat, who was so instrumental in the conversion of their forefathers over fourteen hundred years ago.

No, he is truly out of sight, and out of mind. For is not a memorial which reminds nobody of anything a curious anomaly? It is a page of history in an unknown tongue; a strain of music played to the tone deaf; a mill-wheel, always going never grinding; a clock that neither strikes nor ticks; or anything else absurd and nonsensical that you can think of. It is a contradiction in terms. It is the play of Hamlet without Hamlet. But all along is the fault in the drama or acting, or rather in the audience who are deaf and blind to the presence of the Prince of Denmark? Nay, not only is St. Nuadha forgotten, but as he left behind him no substantial memorial as an inheritance for after times, not even a tombstone, some future Dr. D'Alton may level against him the same argument that in one stroke sweeps out of existence the Fomorians and Nemedians and all the rest of them, and maintain with a great show of impartiality that most probably no such man ever lived, good or bad. Rather is he to be classed " with Jason who sought the Golden Fleece and Aeneas who wandered over land and sea,"[1] as a mere figment of the mind of some early and very imaginative Thackeray or Canon Sheehan. In view of this reasoning such must equally be the fate in store for most of us, if we don't look out. But then, that's no great loss to the world.

The Kildare man, however, must say nothing. His memory is as short as the Roscommon man's. Fulterach, the great Bishop of Clonard (d. 774), for instance, and he built an oratory at Hy Falgia in one of the baronies of Offally, is also for him, as a classicist would say, covered by the waters of Lethe. Of his name and of his retreat —Disert Fulterach—there remains no more trace in his recollection than of last year's snow on Dunmurry Hills, or than of the precious metals that a century and a half ago were mined in its sides, and are now lying there derelict and forgotten.

Equally lost sight of in Kildare are Tullachfobhair, near Naas, and its founder, St. Fechin of the seventh century; Kilbegs, north-west of the same town, and its Knights Hospitallers; Clonagh of St. Fynen,[2] though, as can be established from State Papers, it was in being and flourishing as late as 1396; Killauxaile, where St. Patrick himself founded an abbey for St. Auxil, said by many to have been his nephew, who died there in 454. These names are now all blotted out.[3] They are not to be seen on map or chart. They have disappeared as completely as has St. Finbarr's Round Tower from the city of Cork, or as has

---
[1] " History of Ireland," Vol I., p. 9.
[2] Not to be confounded with Clonenagh of Fintan, in Queen's County.
[3] According to Archdall, Killauxaile or Kill-usaille, became Killussi, which Killossy. At Killossy, which is not far from Kildare, there was a parish church in 1786. We hope and expect there is one there still. So one name is yet to be had (*v. Mon. Hib.* 1st ed., p. 136). A very fine view of the church with its singular Round Tower, engraved in 1792, adorns Grose's Antiquities (II., 84). Another but a poorer one may be seen in Ledwich at p. 155 (2nd. ed.).

a similar beautiful structure from beside Boyle Abbey.[1] They are no more heard in Kildare than the tinkling of St. Evin's consecrated hand-bell is heard in the courthouse of Monasterevin. Kilcock, indeed, still preserves for the student the memory of the Virgin St. Cocha whose feast used to be celebrated on June the 6th. Moone and Timolin [2] indeed remain as the names of two tiny twin roadside villages adjoining one another, and the former also as part designation of a barony. But they are names only. They now recall neither saint nor sanctuary. They are as empty of religious sense or significance in Kildare as the wild birds' nests in the winter hedgerows along the roads.

And how bleak and desolate is a countryside without such memories! It is as if it had been, like the North Pole, always uninhabited; or else as if time were the cruel spirit of Attila, and had crashed over it ruthlessly with devastating hordes. In the eyes of its children, of the lovers of their native heath, how bright and interesting, on the other hand, would it not be had these memories been kept up! Troy is but a ring of sand-dunes, but it is a vast deal more. How interesting might not a countryside become again if even now at the eleventh hour, before all are faded and gone, they were restored and were once more flourishing! Every hill would have its tale, every glen its story to illuminate it. The old chieftain would converse with us from his rath, and the saint would delay a while to teach us a lesson from his dysert! In every county and barony the local historian has in his hands a whistle more potent than Rhoderick Dhu's to people the solitudes, provided only he takes pains and learns how to use it, *and sets about it at once.* The best politics, certainly in the sense of inspiring love and respect for our native land, is the study of the lives of our local saints and sages and chieftains.

The Kildare Archaeological Society, founded in 1891,

---

[1] Twenty years ago, we are informed, a beautiful Round Tower stood near Kilrush, at Querrins, opposite Scattery island. It also is no longer there. The stones were useful, a local gentleman discovered.

The coins were long ago ruthlessly torn out of most of our old ruins.

[2] Originally Tigh-Moling=the house or church of St. Moling. St. Moling (d. 697) was Bishop of Ferns and one of the most remarkable saints of early Ireland. He built another church in Carlow which was also called Tigh-Moling. The latter has been corrupted into St. Mullins.

has, indeed, already done a great deal for this county's past. But its labours are as yet for the most part buried away in great libraries. And it is a pity. For, unlike many of such local societies, it has consistently set its face against the tendency to glorify existing names and families, rather than, by truer and more disinterested work, to shed light and lustre on old pre-Norman Kildare, its clans, its chiefs, its saints, and its civilisation.

Wistfully one reads of the pleasure it was to listen to a king among Irish popular historians whose voice is now still for ever :—

> They who have had the privilege, writes the Bishop of Achonry about the late Archbishop Healy, will not easily forget the delight of sitting beside him on some jutting crag overlooking the numerous islands set in the western sea and hearing him discourse, in choicest phrase, on the religious associations connected with each. The men who fled the vanities of the world and made these lonely islands their homes, the manner of their daily life and its round of prayer and toil, the shrines they built with all their wealth of design and ornament—all were pictured faithfully to the very life, while the listener remained enthralled by the absorbing interest of the narrative.—(*I.E.R.*, July, 1918, p. 18.)

Considered, too, as mere words, Roscommon's Eastersnow has its match in Kildare's Moone. So again the Leinster man had best keep silence. The latter is derived in the same happy-go-lucky fashion as the former, and rivals it in absurdity—in meaning what it does not mean. Moone, contrary to your expectations, and your reminiscences of Old English, has nothing whatever to do with either sun or moon. It comes instead from *moenia* (=ramparts or city walls) ; and thereby hangs a tale ; and a tale it is which is both not a bad instance of the romance of words, and a really good illustration of how our present local nomenclature often obscures, or does its mighty best to blot out, our local history. It is worth while bringing it out.

St. Brigid, according to the legend, once upon a time on her travels through what is now Kildare, came to the place at the present wayside village of Moone, about where now stands the great granite Keltic Cross.[1] So much was she

---

[1] The description of this magnificent Cross (seventeen feet six inches high, from platform to summit, and its roof-like capping stone is gone) was the last

DYSERT

struck with the beauty of the surroundings that she cried out in admiration:
"Glory be to the name of the Lord! Here surely there should be a house dedicated to the praise and service of Almighty God, who has made this country so delightful."

work that the talented Protestant lady, Miss Stokes, did for the antiquities of Ireland. She did not live to complete it, but her notes are published practically as she left them in the *Transactions of the R.I.A.*, Vol. XXXI. (1901). The Cross, and fourteen panels on each side of it, are minutely described; and there are very fine photographs of it from every point of view—half-a-dozen in all. The letterpress includes the story of St. Brigid given above.

No one, it may be noted, can be really learned in Irish literature, or in Irish history and antiquities, as she was, and fail to be sympathetic with Irish faith, sincerity, and civilisation.

The Moone High Cross, by the way, which so delighted one artist enough to appreciate it, was found buried in the Abbey about the year 1835. It was carefully re-erected and in part restored. Illustrations of it may also be seen in O'Neill's "Sculptured Crosses of Ireland," plates 17 and 18.

Similarly the High Cross of Tuam, which dates back to the first half of the twelfth century, and which Petrie considered " the most remarkable of its kind and the most splendid in Ireland " ("Stokes' Life," p. 298), was discovered in 1822 by this distinguished scholar and it broken into three fragments. Two of the fragments were lying in the nettles in the churchyard. The base or pedestal was in the fishmarket beneath a pile of stones and street-sweepings. So, like the Jews of old, the Tuam people were able " to raise stones out of the heaps of rubbish which are burnt."

The two cases are typical both of the vandalism of invasion, and of the utter neglect of our antiquities, at least until recent years, even by those who should know better. Not many years ago an Ogham stone was discovered at Martamane, parish of Killiney, County Kerry. It was being used in a dwelling-house as a lintel over a fire-place, when a man, not a native, went in out of a shower of rain and saw it. A cast of it, most carefully made, is now in the National Museum, Dublin.

Lying beside Moone Cross itself are portions of another and, if anything, a more interesting one. The cross-head was perforated in the centre, chiselled serpents coiled round the perforation. Lord Walter Fitzgerald considers the pattern unique in Ireland and probably exceedingly old (*Journal R.S.A.I.*, December, 1899). Miss Stokes also, in the Kildare Archaeological Journal for the same year, has an article on the symbolic sculpturing of the fragments. They were discovered when a grave was being sunk, and were pitched on the ground beside the Standing Cross. They were there in 1899. Whether they have since been used in building a style, or a cow-house, or are there still, the writer cannot certify.

The Cross of Banagher (King's County) is the worst case yet. Dean Monahan in his " Records of Ardagh and Clonmacnoise "—a work which, besides its great research, is bubbling over with poetry and good nature—tells about it. This Cross he states (p. 366) " had in more prosperous and happy days stood erect beside a crystal spring, which once sent forth its limpid waters in the old market square of Banagher. . . ." Its fate reflects anything but credit on St. Reynagh's ancient town. It bangs Banagher in more than one sense. The crystal spring has ceased to flow. The Cross, thank goodness, is no longer there. About seventy years ago the one and only person—a stranger—who appreciated this beautiful thirteenth century historical and religious monument and who alone, seemingly, could distinguish it from a gate-post, rescued it (all that remained of it) and removed it from amongst, as he describes them, "its brutal and Gothic foes." Once outside of Banagher, it found hundreds to admire it and pity its injuries. They have ever since been banging Banagher. Banged it ought to be. Dean Monahan himself, if he could be brought to say a harsh word about anybody or anything, would not spare it.

St. Columbkille, returned from his banishment or exile in Iona, was at the time at Swords in Dublin. He miraculously heard her cry, and miraculously he replied to her: "Brigid," he answered back, "you may do with the land as if it were your very own by legal right."

A little later he himself reached the spot designated, and on it he established a monastery. He established the monastery, and, as was then the custom, surrounded it with a great stone protecting cashel, as high, perhaps, as was the masonry work round Kilrush Abbey[1] (3½ miles west of Old Seven-gated Kilcullen); or as high as are the walls of Maynooth College or of the Duke of Leinster's demesne, both of which are skirted by the Midland Great Western Railway in the north of Kildare, and very much broader. *Moenia* is a good Latin equivalent for cashel. So this monastery came to be known as Moenia, or Moen-Choluim-Cille. Afterwards it shortened into Moen.

But subsequently some one, an old Anglo-Norman baron most likely, knowing nothing of all this, said to his learned friends: "There now, what was I telling you? Why these Irishries must be an ignorant pack. I believe in my heart they couldn't spell cat. Just look at the way they spell Moone, *M-o-e-n*! We'll spell it right for them." And he did. So Moone it is from that day to this.

And the Kildare man takes with it. The term, of course, is symptomatic of a great, big, carefully enclosed county institution rather than of an ancient home of praise and prayer, founded by a saint and prince of Ireland. But the Kildare man is satisfied. Anything for a quiet life. Ἐν τῳ φρονεῖν γὰρ μηδὲν, ἥδιστος βίος. One is inclined to say of him what, as the story goes, Biddy-the-Basket said of the Dublin Archbishop when, peering through the iron railings, she saw His Grace amusing himself by jumping his Newfoundland dog over his stick : " God love him, but he's aisy plazed." On the other hand, when it is recollected that the name, as a name, is not only a bit of balderdash—that one could tolerate and laugh at—but that it is a misnomer blanketing and smothering up a

---

[1] Erected in the thirteenth century. "It was surrounded by a ditch of great breadth, faced with masonry ten feet high"—(Rawson's *Stat. Survey*). Ditch most probably is here used in its Irish signification—meaning a clay mound —the one bit of partiality to things Irish discoverable in the learned work.

beautiful incident of local history, forthwith we are in quite another mood. Our exclamation suddenly changes into almost as emphatic and uncompromising a condemnation as did the poor apple-woman's the next minute when her friend Judy nudged her on the elbow and whispered : "Whisht, Biddy! Sure tha's not our Archbishup a tall ; tha's the oul' Prodestan' fellah." [1]

Anyway the inhabitants of the little village itself have one consolation : its name has in reality about as much connection with the pale orb of night as has the Hill of Howth with Christmas.

It is worth while adding that when, about the beginning of the fourteenth century it was, the Franciscans came to the same beautiful district, though nothing remained of St. Columbkille's monastery except traces of the cashel or Moenia such as are visible in the old rath to the present day, yet not unnaturally they made their home as near as could be to the place sanctified by the prayers of saints and confessors and the blood of martyrs ; and that, moreover, such is the current practice in every part of Ireland. Many a parish church is apparently not older than sixty or seventy years. But then its site is sacred for hundreds and hundreds. Alas! except that hazy tradition, indistinct as a myth, every other fact in reference to it has very often faded away from the popular memory. We can well sympathise with the old men's angry reluctance to abandon the time-honoured location for one " more convenient and desirable." Their religious instincts are always right.

The custom of calling a parish after its first church—that is after the patron saint or titular of that church—or else after the townland in which this primitive church was built, was practically universal. The latter method, though natural enough, is not much to be admired ; but if a *fait accompli* of olden times, nobody should wish to object to it. Trace it up, and oftentimes the order will be found to be : (*a*) the patron saint of the church, *e.g.*, St. Clare ; (*b*) the

---

[1] " Oh ! what a tarnation oul' fool he is," was, according to Lefanu, who tells the story, and all the weighty authorities, Biddy's second observation. Circumstances alter cases, is a legal maxim.

townland, *e.g.*, Cloonclare (=Clare's lawn or meadow);[1] and (c) the parish, *e.g.*, Cloonclare again (Kilmore); all three derived from the same source. This is ideal. But it is the re-naming, not after an Irish saint nor a saint at all, but after a townland—for instance, Blacklion (diocese of Meath)—or after a town—for example, Enniskillen (Clogher), Kinvara and Clarinbridge (Kilmacduagh)—and the consequent covering up of so much of the parish's history for roughly 800 years that, it is submitted, we should set our faces against. It is this that has already played havoc with such fine old names as Elphin's Desert-Nuadhan, Clogher's Cleenish, Meath's Killpatrick, Bective, Ardbraccan, and Kilbrew, and scores upon scores of others. And the principle is still on the war-path.

We have been told, indeed, of a certain parish whose original designation was compounded of a local martyr's name. The martyr was thus commemorated where above all he should be. Recently a new and stately edifice was erected on a new and magnificent site, where the whole world can see and wonder at it. The incumbent, an excellent priest and a forceful character, has undoubtedly done splendid work. As he often tells them, "When I came among you I found the place of brick, I will leave it of marble." But nothing would do him but improve the parish name as well—improve it out of existence, saint's name and all. He has neither town nor townlet "to himself it may be told," but he insists for the parish on the name of the townland now glorified by his new church. Happily hight, we admit and do not deny, the townland is; let us present it disguised as Lakeview. The ancient name, it seems, with its Irish tang sounded ill and vulgar in his ears. It set his teeth on edge. In his student days he had composed reams of verse, polished and patriotic (published in the Magazines much of it was, too—anonymously); and though a penny bottle of black ink does him now for a

---

[1] There are about 1,800 places in Ireland, whose titles begin with Clon or Cloon. It represents the Irish *Cluain*. Though usually translated as above, its exact meaning is a fertile piece of land surrounded by bog or marsh, or by a bog on one side and water on the other. Its frequent occurrence in our ecclesiastical names is sufficiently explained by the well-known custom of the early Irish saints, to select lonely and retired places for their own habitations, as well as for their religious establishments—(Joyce). This is fully borne out in the instance given in the text.

whole year—but he keeps it corked—still his unatrophied poetic instincts against ill-favoured words and sounds were up in arms. Not for worlds would he imprint on his dainty notepaper such an uncouth address as, say, Ballygurtha. He writing from Ballygurtha! What would his friends think at all?

But the parishioners—when out of his hearing—do not take kindly to the new-fangled title. And the old women can't catch it up right, they complain, and can't get their tongues round it. They call it Like-you, maybe, or Lack-hugh, or Lackennew, or you wouldn't know what. They often vex him—and catch it.[1] And the old men, flustered in his dignified presence, at times forget themselves, and out they blurt the tabooed title. If they would leave it at that, and keep on never minding, they had a chance. But, knowing that he hates it like poison, no sooner does it flash upon their minds that they have put their foot in it, than they get still more 'through other,' and nothing will do them but make bad ten times worse by apologies and vain endeavours to placate him. *Qui s'excuse, s'accuse*, is proverbial; but it is not in their code of diplomacy. And subtle enough that diplomacy is without this maxim. It makes brave efforts to ground the hidden lightning right and left—anywhere, but to draw it and have the skies between themselves and Father Pat serene and unclouded once more.

"God pardon me, and yir Reverence," an old grandfather will exclaim, "for not sayin' your new and purty name. But sure—bad cess be off me!—the oul' wan hopped out on me, so it did, afore ever I found—the peel moral of a wee brattle of a curse—beggin' yir Reverence's pardon—that I'm subject to, on turns, inonst to meself—God forgive me this night and this day!—be manes of them villains of cows that go thievin'. Bad manners to them for cows! Th're born devils.

"But wait till hurself hears of it! She'll scald me, with boilin' water. 'An' above all fornint his Reverence's face,' she'll say, 'An' after all the cautions I gave you when I seen him comin' up the boreen, roulin' on his car. But

---

[1] It is a harder name to say than Lakeview But the above may illustrate their difficulties.

you have no *gumpshin*, not as much as a jinny wran, nor never had. You war ever and always an oul' goose, and that's what you are,'—an' mebbe I am, yir Reverence,—' since the first day I met you,' she'll say, ' an' haven't as much wit or understandin' about you as would take you in out ov the rain. An' its many's the time I toul' you that. To go an' discomposhe his Reverence! An' 'im the most *improvingest* priest—God bless 'im!—we ever had in, in—in the parish. No, we never had the likes of 'im, nor never will.' "

" An' it's true enough, Father Pat. Sure it's wearin' yir goold mitre you ought to be comin' roulin' to a body's doore, an' not yir silk hat, an' will yet, plaze God. Bad luck be off these fly-a-ways ov curates that's goin' now, with their bicycles and their caubeens killin' all the hens of the country ! Shure, as hurself ses, they're more like Prodestan ministers than priests. But why don't ye lay down the law, Father Pat, solid, and make them dress themselves sensible and dacent, the same as they ought, like the oul' men ? It's too aisy ye are, so it is, and has no rules nor regulations to thether them. I misdoubt me, but nothin'll do them next thing but it's up in the elements they'll go with themselves, like a crow, in them new things they do be talkin' about, if ye don't keep an eye on them. God help the poor fellows! for they haven't an ounce."

But it is all no earthly use with Father Pat. And well they are aware of it. He will listen, of course, most politely and attentively to all they have got to say. For the time being, too, he will continue to talk blandly about the crops and the weather. Never a ripple on the surface. But all the same they know in their hearts he won't look the side of the road they are on for a month.

A priest's character, it is to be borne in mind, is canvassed in his little dominion more minutely and astutely than was ever a prime minister's in the cunningest of news sheets. Thank goodness they have the friendly eye which never sees his many real faults. But his little foibles and likes and dislikes are learned and conned by rote by the most unlettered of them ; most sympathetically, we hasten to add, and solely in view of pleasing and humouring him.[1]

---

[1] There is a slang Americanism for this idea—" Jollying."

when the occasion presents itself, and avoiding saying the wrong thing or tramping on his corns. The night before a 'Station' even such an important question as how he likes his eggs boiled for breakfast, whether hard or not, is a matter for deep exploration by the hospitable household, and possibly for the assistance of the parish informational bureau. Their hardy sons and husbands don't care a jot at any time how they get them, hard or soft, provided they do get them; and, of course, they are never asked. But that would never do in this case.

Indeed, we have been informed by his curate, that when Father Pat, soon after his advent to his parish, landed at his first Station-house, the good hostess, having nothing to go upon, was in a quandary. But she was resourceful. She deputed the returned 'Yankee' lady, who had helped in laying the table *à la mode* and curling the napkins into lilies of the valley, and who, having travelled, was considered the " bouldest " personage about, to just go right straight and ask him.

" Would your Reverence be pleased to say," she deferentially inquired in a carefully rehearsed little speech, " how you would wish your eggs done for breakfast ? Do you like them rare or mollified ? "

" Well," he replied, in his own grand way, with just the suspicion of a smile, " if it be not too much trouble I should prefer them mollified."

That ended it. From that day to this he always has had his eggs beautifully 'mollified'. Everybody in the parish knows his taste.

In Ireland we are always proud of our parish. It is the best by long chalks in the " diosey." About that we have no doubt, " no possible probable shadow of doubt, no possible doubt whatever." " You must be a great man when you got here," is a common salute to a new curate. But nobody ever boasts of belonging to Lakeview. They compromise it, and proclaim " I'm from Father Pat's parish." When Father Pat is translated to heaven for all his good works, including building his grand " Catheydrell," we hope the old name will come back. We may rely, it is surmised, on his successor finding out his little mistake. We may also depend upon him, we think, putting up a magnificent stained glass window over the high altar in his honour (it would be so becoming to the church), and having a neat marble slab inserted in the wall beneath it. The present thoroughgoing Ordinary of the parish, Father Pat, will certainly be an Archdeacon, or a Canon anyway, long before then; and the slab will read something like this :—

By the
REV. JOSEPH ANTHONY NEWMAN, P.P.,
AND HIS SORROWING PARISHIONERS
AS A SMALL TOKEN OF THEIR LOVE AND ESTEEM
This Window was erected to the Memory of
The Very Rev. Patrick Canon(?) M———
late lamented Pastor of
LAKEVIEW.
R. I. P.

There will, of course, be as much more inscribed about him and his great doings as there will be place for, and as will not be artistically unsightly. But, that, we trust, will be the last of Lakeview. *Et sic transit gloria mundi.*

Chapter IV

DYSERTS, WHAT THEY WERE

CROAGH PATRICK AND SLIEVE DONARD—MODERN MOUNT MELLERAY—MUNGRET OR MUNGARET ?—KINGSLEY'S "HERMITS" AND BARING-GOULD'S "LIVES OF THE SAINTS."

ON dysert as a word enough attention has perhaps been bestowed; but not more than it deserves, seeing its importance and its frequency of occurrence in Irish place-names. As to what dyserts were in reality, they were of three or four kinds. But this should be said at the outstart, they were all alike in one respect: they were as far removed from the haunts and homes of men as they possibly could be. That was of their very essence. The ruling idea was that of the Thebäid, and the inspiring idea of the Thebäid was that of the Gospel narrative—unhampered and undistracted prayer and communion with God. Most likely, too, the very name was reminiscent of the Gospel text.

"Whilst Canice lived in Aghaboe," writes one of his biographers, "he made his *diserta* in the midst of a swampy marsh between the present Roscrea and Borris-in-Ossory. Here he built a little cell to which he withdrew in Lent and during times of retreat. In after centuries it became a place of pilgrimage."[1]

Manifestly, here again, both saint and pilgrims were treading the path and imitating the example of Him who is for all time the way, the truth, and the life.

Sometimes, then, they were on the sides or the tops of bleak mountains. So Croagh Patrick, rising from the

---

[1] "Footprints of Irish Saints," No. 1, p. 15, *Irish Messenger Series*. The once famous monastery of Aghaboe was built by this saint, who died A.D. 560. For six and a half centuries after him the place was the episcopal seat of the diocese of Ossory.

Connacht sea-shore some 2,500 feet, was selected by our National Apostle. So, too, was the highest peak in Ulster chosen by his disciple, St. Donart. Whether named so or not these were dyserts. Donart built his oratory, writes Colgan, " on the very summit of the mountain itself far from all human habitation."

" Uncomfortable eyries ! " you exclaim with a shudder, as you think of the snows and the pelting rains.

We agree. But please bear in mind that, for those unpampered athletes whose souls were cast in the giant mould of saints, that was their great attraction. They crucified the flesh. And the panorama of sea and plain, lake river and forest, spread before their eyes, was for them a constantly open book, its words written down by a Divine hand. What a book for meditation ! They must have often cried out with the royal psalmist, " How great are thy works, O Lord ! thou hast made all things in wisdom ; the earth is filled with thy riches." " The fool hath said in his heart, There is no God " ; or often exclaimed as did the profane poet,

> " These are Thy glorious works, Parent of good.
> Thyself how glorious then ! "

Uncomfortable, certainly. But those nurtured in such eyries soared nearest to God.

He was a prince-bishop, this Donart, son of Eochy, King of Ulidia. All of his royal race are gone and forgotten. But the name of Slievedonard remains as his own perpetual memorial ; a monument, as it were, raised by his countrymen to his heroic sanctity.

Croagh Patrick's quartzise sides and Slievedonard's granite dome are to-day no less rugged and uninviting than they were fifteen centuries ago. But, except in such intractable places, dyserts generally are, of course, far now from what they were originally, when first their borders were trod by a great and saintly forefather of religious. When a monastery succeeded a solitary's *damliagh* or cell, and was built on even the side of a black and barren mountain, the surroundings, no matter how stern and wild, soon put on a different aspect—transformed by the labours of " the idle monks." The Cistercian Abbey of Mount Melleray is, in our own days, a good example of this. It is nestled amidst gardens and groves, and lawns and fertile pasture lands. In scenic richness it compares not unfavourably with Lismore [1] demesne in view of it on the banks of the Blackwater; or even with Curraghmore [2] in the same county (Waterford), said to be the most beautiful enclosed park in Ireland, and it has 5,000 acres. Yet Mount Melleray's foundations were laid on a bleak slope of the Knockmealdown mountains. In other words, it was planted in a dysert, as was St. Bernard's, the parent house of the Order, at Clairvaux. Visitors observe the untouched and unreclaimed patch of tussocks and brown heather near the Abbey, and contrast it with the adjoining waving corn-fields. They can hardly believe it, that two or three generations ago all the monastery's acres were of the same scraggy pattern. When the Strand, in London, was converted into the Thames Embankment, a perch or so was similarly left as it was. The transformation is no more striking.

Of another class of dyserts, the one to which Dysert-Diarmada, on the now well-ramparted Lerr, perhaps originally bore some resemblance, Mungret on the Shannon, the seaward side of Limerick city, may be taken as typical. A local writer says of it that in the fifth century " and for centuries afterwards, the low-lying corcass lands from the mouth of the Maigue to Limerick were unreclaimed from the Shannon, and the tide ebbed and flowed over this wide expanse, known as 'the lake of Limerick.' So wild was the district around Mungret, and around Limerick to the west, that it was known as *Fasagh Luiminagh*, or the wilderness of Limerick. . . . A sedgy morass is called in Irish *Moing* or *Muing*, which term is also applied to the tall grasses grown in bogs. *Cruit*, a hump, and *Crit*, a back, are words usually applied to round and sloping hills; [hence] *Moing-a-crùit*—the sedgy morass of the sloping hill." [3]

---

[1] King John's Castle here usurps the site of the once famous Lismore, a seat of learning and a school of piety. Over 4,000 students thronged its halls in its palmy days. Among them, it is said, was Alfred the Great of England. History is repeating itself when Mount Melleray College arose in sight of it.

[2] For some good ghost stories in connection with this old seat, see the charmingly written " Lady Anne's Walk," by the daughter of the late Protestant Primate, Dr. Alexander.

[3] Mr. Barry. Quoted in an admirable booklet of the C.T.S. of Ireland— " The Monastery of Mungret," by Father Cahill, S.J.

Moingacruit by an easy and necessary transition has come to be pronounced Mong-a-rit by the people about. The learned Professors, however, in the famous Jesuit College of prophecy do not favour this pronunciation. They call it curtly Mungret. But, seemingly, the simple peasants are, as usual in such matters, right, and the learned Dons wrong. Not to speak of the etymology, the former have the support of generations and generations of native speakers, as well as that of ancient writers, and of the Four Masters. The latter, it is hard to say what authority. We are unprepared, however, to deny that they are acting, as usual with them, on principle. And a principle it is that, more than any other in orthoëpy, curtails, defaces, and " dollops " many a fine word. It is referred to in circles polite as *inertia* or conservation of energy; but by the less refined condensed into one Anglo-Saxon expressive trissyllable, beginning with the letter l. It is unnecessary, we think, to specify it more exactly.

Indeed, as a general rule, the utterance of Irish place-names prevailing in cabin and cottage, is ever so much more correct than that current in hall and mansion. The Maugherow fisherman's Sleggy [1] and Bellashanny, for instance, are the pronunciations of twenty centuries; the National Schoolmaster's Sligo and Ballyshannon are new-fangled anglicisations of yesterday; obscurantist besides, and absurd to boot. Ballyshannon reminds one of the story of Japhet in search of a father. He finds him, but it is the wrong one. At its nearest point the town is thirty good miles away from the lordly river with which its title seeks to claim a paternal connection. Its famous poet, Willie Allingham, made no such mistake in his beautiful " Adieu to Ballyshanny ! " his native town.[2]

In " The Hermits," the hermits of the Cambridgeshire fens, the Rev. Charles Kingsley, a master of the king's English but a very bigoted anti-Catholic, gives a very graphic picture of what these marshy dyserts were like.

---

[1] Well named from Sligeach, the shelly river. The town itself is not old.
[2] The schoolmaster's Ballyshannon is bad in every part; the last, the worst. The fisherman correctly pronounces Bel-atha-Seanaigh=The mouth—of the ford—of Shannagh. It is so called by the annalists. Bally is a corruption of baile, a town. But the spot was called Bellashanny centuries before a town arose on it. Some English words do " change their parents," but the change is always a result of ignorance.

The description leaves such a clear impression that another Protestant clergyman, the Rev. S. Baring-Gould, M.A., quotes and adopts it in a corresponding work of his. The title of the second work may equally surprise the reader who is unaware of good and learned Anglicans' nervous anxiety to claim as many of our old anchorites as ever they can as their very own—" The Lives of the Saints." Ireland in far back ages was so thickly covered with forest that it was called (spelling it phonetically) *Inis-na-vivy*, the Island of the Woods. The Irish and English boglands and morasses, at the period, had, too, we may be sure, very much of a family likeness. Hence the description will equally apply to the former; to *Fasagh Luiminagh*, for instance, and to *Corcach-mor-Mumhan*, or the Great Marsh of Munster, to which we shall refer later on, quite as well as to Ramsay or to Croyland.

> The Fens of the seventh century, [writes Kingsley], were probably very like the forests at the mouth of the Mississippi or the swampy shores of the Carolinas. Their vast plain is now, in summer, one sea of golden corn; in winter, a black dreary fallow cut into squares by stagnant dykes, and broken only by unsightly pumping mills and doleful lines of poplar trees. Of old it was a labyrinth of black wandering streams; broad lagoons; morasses submerged every spring-tide; vast beds of reeds and sedge and fern; vast copses of willow, alder, and grey poplar, rooted in the floating peat, which was swallowing up slowly, all devouring, yet all preserving, the forests of fir and oak, ash and poplar, hazel and yew, which had once grown in that low, rank soil, sinking slowly (so geologists assure us) beneath the sea from age to age. Trees, torn down by flood and storm, floated and lodged in rafts, driving the waters back upon the land. Streams, bewildered in the flats, changed their channels, mingling silt and sand with peat moss. Nature, left to herself, ran with wild riot and chaos, till the whole fen became one Dismal Swamp . . . [But] there are islands in the sea which have escaped the destroying deluge of peat moss—outcrops of firm and fertile land which in the early Middle Ages were so many natural parks, covered with richest grass and stateliest trees, swarming with deer and roe, goat and boar, as the streams around swarmed with otter and beaver, and with fowl of every feather, and fish of every scale.
>
> Beautiful after their kind were those fair isles in the eyes of the monks who were the first settlers in the wilderness. The author of 'The History of Ramsay' grows enthusiastic, and

somewhat bombastic also, as he describes the lonely isle, which got its name from the solitary ram who had wandered thither, either in extreme drought or over the winter ice, and, never able to return, was found feeding among the wild deer, fat beyond the wont of rams.

Kingsley's sketch is embodied in the Life of St. Guthlac in Vol IV.—Vol. IV., that for April, of the Rev. Baring-Gould's twelve volumes on the " Lives of the Saints!" Of the touching of the first monk at Mungaret there has been traced no record. But we cannot be far astray if we imagine it as something similar to the landing of Guthlac at Croyland, in Lincolnshire, though the latter happened many, many, years later. Dane and Norman, time and utter neglect, have dealt hardly indeed with our Irish books and MSS.; but this is taken from authentic English sources by the painstaking clergyman-author.

Guthlac, a youth of high family, had renounced, like St. Martin, the profession of arms. At the time (c. A.D. 714)[1] he was looking out for a place of penance and of lonely retirement. The churl Tatwin, whom he met, told him of an island " which oftentimes men had attempted to inhabit, but none had succeeded, on account of manifold horrors and fears and the loneliness of the wild wilderness. . . . He embarked in a boat, and they rowed through the wild fens till they came to the spot called Crow or Croyland, which was so lost in the marsh that few knew of it except Tatwin. . . . It was on St. Bartholomew's Day that Guthlac came crashing through the reeds of the morass to the island which was to be henceforth his home for life."

Equally unpromising, no doubt, was the *Cruit*, or sloping hill, standing like an island in the midst of Fasagh Luiminagh,[2] that is the wilderness of Limerick. There Nessan, " the Deacon of Mungairit," as the Martyrology of Donegal entitles him, established his home. It was about two

---

[1] So the Rev. Baring-Gould. Abbot, now Cardinal, Gasquet would place the date earlier by about thirty years. The subsequent history of Crowland from 716 when Ethelwold, King of the Mercians, brought the Benedictines to it, till 1539 when John Bridges, the last Benedictine Abbot, was expelled and died far away from his ancient home, the Cardinal sketches in his beautiful work, " The Greater Abbeys of England " (p. 62 etc.). An aisle of its splendid monastery church was then purchased for £26. It still remains.

[2] Or Luimneach (pr. Liminegh). It is the old name of this portion of the Shannon. The *n* in it changed, as in many other instances, to *r*, and the -*ch* at the end, as is also not uncommon, hardened into -*ck*. Hence Lime*r*i*ck*.—(Joyce)

centuries before Guthlac "crashed through the reeds" to Croyland, and hundreds and hundreds of years before the city of Limerick was dreamt of. The home grew into a monastery, and Nessan, if not the first settler on the *Cruit*, was at least the first Abbot of Mungaret. Subsequently, as Aubrey de Vere writes,

> " Centuries ten
> It stood, a convent round it as a star,
> Forth sending beams of glory and of grace
> O'er woods Teutonic and the Tyrrhene sea."

Father Cahill, S.J., himself speaks of Mungaret in prose as beautiful as the poetry with which he introduces his unpretentious booklet :—

> Like all the great old Celtic schools of Ireland, it had its abbot and its saints, its poets and artists and scholars; and trained and sent forth its missionaries to teach the nations centuries before the Normans set foot in Britain. Before the mighty nations that now sway the destinies of the world had yet emerged from barbarism; before the languages and the literatures which are now the world's richest secular inheritance were yet born, science and literature were cultivated on Shannon's banks, and pupils from England and Germany and far-distant Italy came there to seek what no place else in Europe could supply. The languages of Greece, Rome and Palestine were taught to apt disciples, and the heroes of the Aeneid and the Iliad were compared with Cuchullin and the Red-branch warriors of our own Irish bards.

Chapter V

THE LAKE DYSERT

DEVENISH AS AN EXAMPLE—STONE CHURCHES AND LL.D. "ANTIQUARIANS"

THE island in the lake was a third class of dysert. It was first favourite among the early Keltic saints. Those hallowed spots, their surfaces covered with old ruins, are found in the majority of the thirty-two counties, in some counties many of them. Devenish, Inismacsaint, etc., in Fermanagh, Trinity in Cavan, Church Islands in both Lough Melvin and Lough Allen in Leitrim, Iniscaltra or St. Camin's Holy Island in Galway, Saint's Island and Inchmore of Kieran and Columbkille in Longford—these are a few of them. In the estuary of the Fergus, practically a lake, in Clare, there is a group of them.

The first mentioned, Devenish, is an example quite as good as any. It may serve to show both what they were like and what was their fate.

When Molaise, the friend of Aidan of Cavan afterwards of Ferns, made off this peaceful place amidst the magnificent scenery of Lough Erne, he exclaimed :

"Good is the discovery we have made,
A broad lake with mountain and field!"

This happened about the year 530, for the saint died in 563. The Druids tried to expel him but failed. His monastery, according to Cardinal Moran, became the most famous in the kingdom.[1]

The most ancient structure on Devenish was that called

---

[1] V. Moran's Edition of Archdall. On it we rely for our main facts. Standish O'Grady's *Silva Gadelica* also contains a very nice life of St. Molaise, "one of the twelve Apostles of Ireland." It is translated from a sixteenth century MS. in the British Museum. But Moran's Archdall contains almost all the facts given in the *Silva*.

the House of Molaise. The Round Tower, according to experts, is of the ninth or tenth century, but this was far older. Possibly, nay likely, it was the identical building that sheltered Molaise himself thirteen, almost fourteen, centuries ago. It looked such an age. It was a small rectangular, stone-covered structure of high-pitched roof, its square-headed doorway on the western end. The walls were of great thickness, built of large stones in the Cyclopean style. It bore a general resemblance to the oratory of Gallerus at Smerwick Harbour in Kerry, not improbably the oldest house in Ireland. Within the memory of Fermanagh men of the last generation this house was standing almost perfect. To-day, by good searching, you may discover its dwarf walls overtopped by the nettles.

In Ledwich's " Antiquities " there is a splendid engraving —in the work the engravings are all splendid (they were not his), the letterpress as bad as bad can be—representing Devenish as it was in 1793, the date of the publication of the massive volume (2nd Edition). A visitor to-day, comparing it with what it was even then, must come to the conclusion that time alone never wrought such havoc. It was vandalism pure and simple. Devenish is too near Enniskillen town, and, we have been told, it served as an excellent quarry. One of its ancient oratories was covered on the outside with cut stone. It was stripped and the stones boated away to flag Enniskillen Protestant Church.[1] There, we believe, they are yet. This latter is the house of worship about which Dean Swift made the cynical couplet, whose first line runs—

" Low church and high steeple,"

its second, a neat deduction from these two features as incongruous as any pair of names that ever were coupled together in the Skellig Lists, of the character of the Enniskillen people. Whatever it be, appreciation of old times and old manners in the Maguire country, is scarcely to be reckoned among their shining virtues.

The baptismal font of the island's great Abbey Church, rebuilt by Prior O'Flanagan in 1449, now adorns the modern

---

[1] Wakeman, *Journal Royal Historical and Archaeological Association*, January, 1874, and he was an Enniskillen man.

and tasteful Catholic Church of Monea [1] on the eastern shores of Lough Erne, Irish-Romanesque as to its architecture and appropriately dedicated to St. Molaise. Unlike a more exquisitely sculptured font, that of old monastic Clonard, in which Molaise was educated and trained to piety, it is there put to its proper use. The more artistic one is placed in the Protestant church of Clonard, a church constructed, Dr. Healy believes, in part out of the remains of the Round Tower, which has totally disappeared from beside it, and "a plainer and uglier building than such edifices usually are in Ireland"—unless, of course, they are 'appropriations.' The font stands, like a manifest intruder, awkwardly before the Communion Table. "It is quite evident," is the Archbishop's comment, "that the worthies who placed it there knew little of ancient Christian usages." [2]

---

[1] We should like to believe that this district borrows its name from the lady Monoa, of the royal stock of Tara and Cashel, who was Molaise's mother. But authorities are against us. Laserian, by which her sainted son is often referred to, is not, by the way, a translation of Molaise. It is really the same name. The prefix Mo- (*cf.* French *Mon Père*) of which the latter is deprived is compensated for by an affix, which has a similar force in Gaelic. Hence we can see the mistake that Mr. Trimble the author of the "History of Enniskillen," recently published, falls into when he states (I. 24), "The Abbey at Devenish was founded (says Archdall, p. 259) by St. Laserian, and others say it owes its origin to Saint Molaise." The mistake is inexcusable since, at the very page in the edition quoted from, and in the very sentence relied on, Archdall says that St. Laserian is "called also Molaisse." The author is one of the best informed men in Fermanagh ; an *alumnus* of Portora which overlooks Devenish ; has lived all his life beside it. That such a mistake is possible with such a man is not, we hope, a fair index to the knowledge about the noble sanctuary among the rank and file of Enniskilliners.

There are two other noted Irish saints of the same name, Molaise of Ferns and Molaise of Inishmurray. In Fermanagh, Leitrim and Sligo, it is pronounced Mŏlósh, the first *o* very slender, or hardly heard. As a Christian name it is as Irish as the *ceannabhán*. Perhaps owing to this, two or three bearing it are as many as you may expect to meet in a lifetime. An Enniskillen merchant, who knows everybody for twenty miles around, assures us there is not one of the name coming into the town. We believe him.

Enniskillen does take its name from a woman, but one of a totally different stamp, Kethelinda or Kethlenn, wife of the Fomorian sea-robber, Balor of the Mighty Blows, and by all accounts something of a terror herself. Enniskillen= (anciently) Innis-Cethlenn=the Island of Kethelinda.

As a town though it dates only from 1612 yet, as the author just mentioned shows, it is found spelt in thirty-two different ways. This should create no surprise. Until the advent of Johnson's Dictionary (1755), common English words were spelt almost any way. Enniskillen is a Plantation town, planted in what Sir John Davys 300 years ago described as "the fattest and richest soil in all Ulster," the Maguires having been duly hanged, and subsequently duly calumniated and caricatured.

[2] In the vestry of Kells (Meath) Protestant church, surrounded as it is by two or three ancient Keltic Crosses (one of them unique) and a Round Tower, are preserved as curios several Catholic sacred vessels. Amongst them is shown an ingeniously constructed silver (or pewter) drinking tankard ! Most likely it once graced an old Kells inn. In a certain public museum in this country the

THE LAKE DYSERT 37

At the dissolution of the monasteries, the possessions of the Devenish communities were tabulated with most scrupulous exactness, with a view to honest legal robbery. There is no mention in the tabulations of the saints' relics—the relics of Paul, of Peter, of Laurence the Martyr and of the Martyr Stephen, of Mary, of Martin, " of other illustrious saints' relics a great share, and some relics of the holy successors [of Peter] that were sepulchred in Rome "—nor of " the load of Rome's soil " soaked with the blood of the Coliseum martyrs. These were the gems and jewels that St. Molaise had brought back with him from the Eternal City and deposited in his beloved Devenish to consecrate and sanctify it, as the sixteenth century MS. in the British Museum testifies,[1] and as tradition supports. Doubtless they were considered of no commercial value. Yet at an inquisition taken near Enniskillen, 18th September, 1609,[2] even such petty details were solemnly written down as that out of the island's 'herenagh land' the bishop of Clogher in right of his bishopric was entitled to " eight days coshiere in his visitation and for want of flesh or wine, or aquavite, four shillings sroaghans [stroans or bannocks] of oatbread, and a beef per annum." It was also ' found ' that " the said abbey, with one orchard and more [the orchards are never forgotten], are situate on the island of Devenish " and out of this the said bishop of Clogher " had yearly a refection for a day, or ten shillings in lieu thereof, and not else, but not to stay all night."

This is high testimony to the goodness and flavour of the Devenish apples. It is likewise high testimony to the confiscators' carefulness in clutching at every scrap and stock and stone of Catholic ecclesiastical property, the endowments of Catholic piety for ten or eleven centuries. In many cases this property was handed over to the newlight churchmen as a consideration for looking after our souls. But after the legal transference they bothered themselves no further. They did not even take the trouble to

---

writer also observed a sacred oil-stocks. It was labelled "A Pyxis." It is offensive to Catholic feeling to have such things in such places at all. It is to be hoped that our National Ecclesiastical College will some day have its own National Ecclesiastical Museum, and soon.
[1] *Silva Gadelica*, pp. 29 and 31.
[2] Mr. Trimble gives 1670 as the date for this or for a similar Inquisition (p 25.)

learn the language in which alone they could speak to the people. " They sought not us but ours." [1] The magnificent monastery churches they gutted, and then left to wreck and ruin. Further, it is high testimony to the labours of the poor evicted communities. Devenish, *Insula Bovium* [2] or Ox Island it is interpreted, when King Conall Derg about 530 made a gift of it to his royal friend, Molaise, was not indeed bleak and barren like the side of Knockmealdown mountain when the Cistercians acquired the rights of it, " the rents to be paid to-morrow." But, as those monks of our own days turned the scraggy moorlands into deep pastures, so they converted the ox-lands into terraced gardens and rich orchards.

And there was something uncanny, or we may say reminiscent of prophecy, about the produce of those orchards, the Devenish apples. For to his mother, Monoa, in a vision of the night was foreshadowed the greatness of her yet unborn child, destined to be the founder of Devenish ; and it was symbolised to her as a magnificent apple which dwarfed all others. She had found, she imagined, seven sweet apples. But than the best of them gold was not so beautiful, nor could she hold it in her hand for its bulk. As such was Molaise among his contemporaries.

No Enniskillen youngsters are ever known to steal down to Devenish in the protecting gloaming, and none to stay there all night. The orchards are all gone. A few perennial flowers still haunt the place, but there is not a crab-tree on the whole island. Its tower and the skeletons of its dilapidated churches stand there still, gaunt and fearsome, like ghosts of the past. It is a sad past. But it is a most edifying and glorious past.

Not to speak again of those already mentioned, Longford has its ancient Devenish in Inchcleraun (=Inis Clothrann)

---

[1] The expression is Dr. Kelly's, " Dissertations on Irish Church History," p. 288. He amply justifies it. " The ' Reformation,' " writes a Protestant Englishman, " from its very outset had plunder written on its front, but as to Ireland it was all plunder from the crown of its head to the sole of its foot."—Cobbett's "'History of the Reformation," Cardinal Gasquet's ed., p. 268.
[2] " Beatissimus Lasreanus . . . construxit clarissimum monasterium in stagno Herne, nomine Daimhinis, qui sonat latine Bovis insula."—An ancient Life of St. Aidan.

or the Island of the Seven Churches [1] in Lough Ree; Westmeath, its Devenish in Inchbofin where a monastery was founded about 450 by St. Rioc, said to be the custodian of St. Patrick's books; Kerry, its Devenish in beautiful Innisfallen. These, too, are but a few examples. Scores are unnoticed. Temples and cloisters and ancient houses of all of them met with similar vandalism; and the ruins, monuments, even as such, of the culture of ages gone by no less than of the piety, were again ruined by further vandalism. These gone, the "ferociously prejudiced" Ledwich and the whole Trinity College ascendancy pack could blatter freely through ponderous tomes about the barbarism of the Irish until their friends, the Anglo-Normans, appeared on the scene. Except a scholar, who could gainsay them? The sacred islands belong now to men whose names are neither Murphy nor O'Kelly. Their title deeds if traced back will be found based on similar inquisitions and on precisely the same legal plundering. *Ex uno disce omnes.*

"Ferociously prejudiced," by the way, as just applied to the well-known author strikes you as a rather hasty epithet, does it? Well, it is not a bit of it. It is more than justified. Further, as intimated in the printing of it, it is not ours. It is that of a writer who most carefully weighs his words, and who as an authority is as good as there is—the present learned President of the Royal Society of Antiquaries (Ireland).[2] Ledwich's school of antiquaries he describes as the Danish. For if anything indicating culture, from a Round Tower to a church window of delicate tracery, manifestly ante-dating the period mentioned, was found, they forthwith ascribed it to the Danes! With them no good could come out of Nazareth. Even the humble forts that crown the hills, homesteads and castles of our pagan and early Christian forefathers to be found by the score where a Northman's foot never trod, they set down as Danish!

They had even the cool audacity to declare that till

---

[1] Its oldest church, Temple-Diarmid, had a square belfry, and its bell could, it is said, be heard seven miles. This almost unique belfry still exists. St. Diarmid was, according to Father McGivney ("Place-Names of Longford") a brother of St. Felim, the patron of Kilmore diocese.
[2] Presidential Address, 1916, p. 22.

the Anglo-Norman invasion stone churches were unknown in Ireland. That this cannot be sustained may at once be fairly inferred from both what has just been said in this chapter, and from what will be said in the succeeding one. The specific absurdity is not dead yet. Dilettanti in archaeology now and then trot it out. For its thorough refutation we would refer the reader, if he has not Petrie's works, to either the *Dublin Review*, September, 1845, or else to an admirable little pamphlet, "The Round Towers," by " S. J.,"[1] Belfast, 1886, p. 61 etc. Smaller, or rather less important—for they were all small—sacred edifices, it is true, were generally constructed of wood up till the twelfth century; but from St. Patrick's time onward the larger ones were of stone. A lie which has a fibre of truth is always the hardest lie to kill. It is like a Scotch thistle. Tramp on it. It is up again before you find, and four heads on it this time. This calumny is not a bad instance.

Flann of Monasterboice, writing early in the eleventh century, gives the names of three masons—" Caeman, Cruitnech, and Luchraid strong," " good was their intelligence "—who belonged to St. Patrick's household. " They made *damliags* first in Erin; eminent their history." he subjoins. Should we accept Ledwich's or the dilettanti's opinion those master masons of " the good intelligence," Messrs. Caeman, Cruitnech, and Luchraid strong, must have had an easy time of it.

By great courtesy the *chiaroscuro* of lies and truth, which went under the name of Irish Antiquities—if not posing as ' Polite Literature '—in and before Dr. Ledwich's time and up to the advent of Petrie, may be allowed to be called a science. But if so, it should never be lost sight of that it was the one science in which a man might say what he liked and prove it as he willed. Imagination rather than cold reason was his divinity. Moreover, provided that he either had appeared voluminously enough in print, or was a General, a D.L., or an LL.D., he was, *eo ipso*, accepted as an authority not to be questioned. Reversing T. à Kempis' advice, attention was rather paid to who said a thing than to what was in it. A social position, or a title of scholarship, if not worth in reality a Chicago degree, dazzled and

---

[1] Mr. John Salmon, Belfast.

charmed away all criticism. In this, as a general description, there is unfortunately little exaggeration. That day is gone. It is a blessing. But the absurd, splendidly brought out tomes, Vallancey's, Ledwich's, and the rest of them, remain. Worse still, they are practically the only books dealing specifically with the subject to be had at all. Hence largely amateurs' mistakes.

Damliag or *diambliag*, mentioned above, is pronounced duleek. Ancient Irish Glossaries define it to be an edifice of stone. By native writers the term is applied, *par excellence*, to a cathedral or to an Abbey church. Here we have accounted for the title of the Meath town on the Nanny Water, as well as of Meath's two eastern baronies. The annotations of Tirechan on the book of Armagh, one of our oldest authorities, assert that a church—a stone one, of course—was built at Duleek by St. Cianan (or Keenan) in A.D. 490. Lest we should have any doubt about it the Office of St. Cianan in Cambridge library explains the name in precisely the same way. The church belonged to the Abbey he founded there (v. *Dublin Review, loc. cit.*). The place still contains a monastery's ruins. So Duleek in its history is Dysert-Diarmada over again.

Chapter VI

THE OCEAN DYSERT

SKELLIG MICHAEL—MODERN CALDEY—OLD WORLD MUSEUMS
—ARDOILEN—BISHOP'S ISLAND.

" With [Thee] conversing I forget all time ;
All seasons and their change, all please alike."
—MILTON, P.L., Bk. IV. 1. 639.

THE lake home was indeed an ideal asylum for prayer and contemplation. But the ideal of ideals was the island in the ocean. Surely there, if anywhere, the religious who fled from the world, if he could be said at all to be still in it, was not of it.

The west coast of Ireland from Donegal to Kerry is dotted, we should rather say gemmed round, with such dyserts, all as such of the sixth or seventh century. Taking them in order from Donegal to Kerry, we have Tory Island of St. Columba in the extreme north, ten miles from anywhere ; Inishmurray of St. Molaise, off the coast of Sligo, it has often and exhaustively been written about ; Inishglora of St. Brendan the Navigator in the foaming Atlantic beyond Mayo ; the two Inishkeas, or St. Kea's Islands, a little further south ; Ardoilen or High Island of St. Fechin, west of the most westerly point of Connemara ; St. Macdara's Isle further south, within view of Connemara's most southerly headland ; the Aran Isles of St. Enda,[1] the great breakwater of neglected Galway Bay ; Bishop's Island not far from old Kilkee in Clare ; Inishtooskert of St. Brendan, and three or four of Blasquet's dozen isles (the hen with

---

[1] Columbkille's " Farewell to Aran," one of this poet-saint's finest pieces, has been beautifully translated by Hyde. We can only give a stanza :—
" O Ara, darling of the West,
Ne'er be he blest who loves not thee,
Herdless and childless may he go
In endless woe his doom is dree."
—*Lit. History of Ireland*, p. 195.

her flock of chickens) belonging to north Kerry; Skellig Michael or St. Michael's Rock, off Bolus Head in a more southern promontory, of the same county; and many more.

The two first mentioned, Tory and Inishmurray, and also some of the Aran Isles, are fairly large in extent. But these alone. One characteristic common to all of them is, difficulty of access. That indeed is implied in the very prefix *Inis-*. According to O'Donovan it comes from *inse*, hard to get at. This feature should be well noted, as it plays an important part in their history.

St. Michael's Rock, or the Greater Skellig is a good example of them. It is 714 feet high. In the distance it looks like an enormous pillar standing amidst the waters. On a nearer view, as you sail to it, it is

> like some huge cathedral, its spires rising over 600 and 700 feet, respectively, above the sea. Passing into the smoother water, under its lee, we see the round roof of its cells, 540 feet above us, clinging to the ridge like swallows' nests, the most western of Christ's fortresses in the ancient world. It was dedicated to St. Michael, as if the storm-swept peak filled the monks with greater dread than usual of his vanquished opponent, ' the Prince of the power of the air '; so also did their brethren dedicate the sea-girt rocks of St. Michael, off the coasts of Normandy and Cornwall, to the warlike Archangel. . . . A little cove, ending in a vast and gloomy cavern, and guarded by a tower-like rock, forms the landing place, only to be used in favourable states of the wind, for the waves often rise and fall for twenty feet up the rock. . . . Even the prosaic State Papers (under January, 1584) speak of this coast ' where the ocean sea raiseth such billows as can hardly be endured by the greatest ships.'

This description is from the exact pen of the present President of the Royal Society of Antiquaries (Ireland).[1] In 1891 that learned body visited the Skellig Rocks. But though conveyed in " a great ship " enough, a heavy gun-boat, the Atlantic rollers were too much for them, and almost all of them, as it was delicately put, succumbed to the sea-gods. Even learned men, we understand and it is a satisfaction to know it, are after all quite as human as any of us. They were only able—afterwards—to descant on the impressive view, " the jagged rocks and pinnacles, and the

---

[1] *Journal R.S.A.I.*, Vol. VII., fifth series, p. 307.

dazzling spray, and the great green billows rushing round their base, and the glorious sunshine"—and so on, and so on, in the choicest of phrases. It was for them Yarrow Unvisited.

But on June 10th, 1897, in a summer outing the same Society sailed again to the Skelligs in the good ship *Caloric*. The steamer was stouter, or else the sea gods were more propitious, and they had a very pleasant five hours on the tip-top of St. Michael's Rock. For to men deeply versed in the subject of antiquities Skellig Michael is a little paradise—for about five hours but no longer. They examined the cashel skirting the very edge of the precipices; and the corbell-roofed cloghauns or stone houses; and the church and the oratories, one of them with an inlaid cross of white stone; and the tiny cemetery with its rude crosses and its cross-scribed slabs bedded in cushions of sea-pink; and the pinnacle that shows up on the southern bluff like the Great Stone Face about which Nathaniel Hawthorne writes, or is it a mighty cross rudely chiselled towering above the whole island? And they were delighted with everything. For were they not revelling in the past, the dusky past of the year 600 or 700, the long, long, past that was there before their eyes? A journey of a few hours in space had taken them back twelve centuries at least in time. And as some of them, tired at last, sat round on weathered blocks, and ate their ham-sandwiches and drank their nice hot thermo-flasked tea, they tried to fancy on what the poor monks fared in these early centuries on that barren rock. Was it on shell-fish, or on sea-weed or 'dillisk,' or what?

"They must have had a lot of fast days," said one.

"Not often a five-course dinner," said another.

"Not many of them as robust-looking, I fear, as Macaulay's fat Derry man," exclaimed a third.

"There are the Colettines," said a lady of the party, "when they are starving they ring a bell. A cousin of mine was sailing in her father's yacht down the Boyne when she heard it, and nothing would do her but go and join them. Just think of that! We all tried to stop her, but it was no earthly use. But what use, in the name of goodness, would a bell be here were it as loud as the Round Tower bell of Ardmore, County Waterford, that could be heard eight miles off, in this un-get-at-able place?"

"How uncomfortable it must have been in the winter time!" observed another.

"Well yes, certainly," replied the lady. "Not very khushi, certainly. No roaring fires to gather around but roaring storms. But then these saints of old," and here she laughingly ostentatiously carried to a less rough boulder the soft silk cushion that the gentleman who had just spoken had cavalierly insisted on carrying up for her from the *Caloric*. "Those anchorites in their stone bee-hives," she resumed, "with their stone stools and stone forms, were made of steel as hard as, as—these rocks. They did not woo comfort, like most of us, with all the assiduity of the domestic cat. Not they!"

But amidst the joking and bantering, and the lady never stopped once she began, they all agreed that the sixth, seventh and eighth century recluses were super-men, heroic men.[1]

A quiet member of the group very happily quoted Dr. Johnson's well-known observations on his visit to Iona :—

> Far from me and from my friends be such frigid philosophy as may conduct us indifferent and unmoved over any ground which has been dignified by wisdom, bravery, or virtue. That man is little to be envied whose patriotism would not gain force on the plain of Marathon, and whose piety would not grow warmer amidst the ruins of Iona.

The quotation was loudly applauded, and he had to say it over again—a genuine encore. "Exactly my sentiments," declared the lady. "I would have repeated the lines only I forgot them. I have always had myself the greatest respect for these old islands, and would canonize every ascetic of them if I had my way."

Athletes of Christ, the old chroniclers call them, and their doings are habitually described in terms taken from

---

[1] The non-Catholic leader of the excursion, with a broadmindedness that can appreciate everyone's point of view—a feature that is indeed very marked in all the members of this cultured Irish body—had written of "this deserted little 'city of God'":—

"It seems so very lonely, so very far from even that quiet world, whose blue grey and purple headlands bound the eastern view, that it takes little stretch of the imagination to see what a city of refuge such a place must have been to ardent self-conscious men fleeing from the temptations of the great cities and decaying civilisation of the old world, and even from the missionary labours of men of the type of Columbanus, to fight with such sin as they brought with them, unstrengthened by the evil outside them."—The Excursion *Guide*, p. 42.

the arena and the wrestling ring. What cared they for the world, or its wealth, or its opinions, or its conventions, or its honours? Their one ambition, to serve Christ, and faithfully follow His most difficult counsels. Anything and everything else was to them a matter of absolute indifference. Their aims and objects—to borrow a beautiful simile we recently came across—were like crystal waters sweeping aside the muddy currents of life.[1]

Even recent years have occasionally witnessed something not very dissimilar; something, too, which helps us realise that " truth can stand against the world." For, as the essayist continues, " it outlives it and blooms immortally." [2] We may give the instance which St. Michael's Rock recalls.

Caldey is a lonely island off the stormy southern Welsh coast. From about A.D. 500 till 1000 it had been a Keltic monastic island, and from 1113 till 1534 again monastic. At this last date all monasteries in the British Isles were 'dissolved,' that is, wrecked. Fanaticism itself abashed would have felt—to use Milton's words—" how awful goodness is," and shrunk from invading such peaceful islands consecrated to retirement and prayer. But there was precious little religious fanaticism about the English 'reformation.' The cool calculating zeal of plunder they could not escape. So Caldey went down with the rest.

But quite in our own times, no farther back than 1906, a colony of devout Anglican monks, Oxford and Cambridge graduates, some of them of the bluest blood in England as our forgotten ones were of the noblest families in Ireland, with not a little of the same spirit again settled down in Caldey. The Established Church, its prejudices against celibates long since evaporated, was proud of them; and assistance poured in to make their chosen home as bright as wealth could make it. But their spirit rose superior to it all. The unseen influences of the holy men of the days gone by were about them. They searched their bibles. They studied and they prayed and, the grace of God assisting, at the end of seven years they were one and all safe once more in the fold of Peter. To-day they form a Catholic Benedictine community of the strictest observance. They

---

[1] " The Candle of Vision," by A.E. Macmillan, 1919.
[2] " Proverbial and Moral Thoughts," by C. H. Hanger, p. 15.

sacrificed friendships and endowments. Not knowing where on the morrow to get their daily bread, for conscience' sake they stepped down from assured affluence to misery and poverty as did their prototypes the recluses of St. Michael's Rock, Inishmurray, and all the rest of those ocean dyserts, more than a thousand years before them.

"So nigh is grandeur to our dust,
So near is God to man,
When duty whispers low, 'Thou must'
The youth replies, 'I can!'"

So, resuming its 900 years' history, Caldey is once more a Catholic monastic island.

And quite correctly indeed the lady of the " trippers " described Skellig Michael as ungetatable. How many of the party of eighty-three, we may ask, would have sailed for it had they to go, not in a luxurious screw steamer, but in Connemara curraghs? Such and no better were the seventh century boats. It was equal to a novice-ship to enter the sheltering cove at all. And granted that our excursionists so reached it, safe and sound and enjoying life, the sea gods being very propitious, how many of those, we wonder, who went jauntily enough up the new corkscrew road, blasted it is through the solid rock to the lighthouse, would have mounted up the 670 slippery steps roughly cut in the face of the cliff—almost as straight as the Eiffel Tower it is—poetically sublime though the ascent would be; the sea-birds whirling far below as you looked down; and, lower still, the trampling waves now thundering up the crags, now " falling back in cascades and threads of silver," now seething as in a maelstrom at their rocky feet; and paradise of the antiquary though the summit would be, when at last they attained it, by this the sole way? We live in softer times. Lifts and cushions are more to our liking than such breathless and fearsome, if noble, climbing.

All these sacred islands are practically equally difficult of approach. Inishtooskert, for instance, has almost perpendicular walls 573 feet high. Ardoilen[1] is worse. For

---

[1] Well named, of course, in Irish, and well translated for a wonder into English as High Island. Such really good translations are as rare as blackberries in November. But like such blackberries, too, they should be discarded. There is no use for them.

the Atlantic breakers have eaten well into it, and its cliffs overhang. It is a feat to be as proud of as scaling a pinnacle of the Alps to enter it at all. To Inishmurray you could row the short four miles from Stredagh Point of a very fine day in about an hour. But should the wind be blowing, however gently from any part, you would be lucky if you reached it at all. This the clever islanders well know, and even the prying revenue men have at last learned to reckon with it. An Aran visit, is a phrase current in Galway, and a good one. Watch the weather and you can boat it to Aran easily enough. As to coming away again, well, perhaps in a week you risk it, perhaps in a month. You take your chances. But anywhere else, unless there were ' great expectations' indeed, your welcome would very likely be long worn out.

But, let them be as they will, it is in no wonder at all that learned historians and archaeologists who only with reluctance and many misgivings borrow statements second-hand out of books, but always go down when they can to the bedrock of authority, haunt these spots. For here are natural truth-telling museums of the sixth and seventh centuries, almost as untouched by the hands of man as a geological Devonian stratum. An enthusiastic Irish antiquary of our days acquired an old castle at Ardglass. He reconstructed it, equipped it with everything antique, and has it exactly as it was in its heyday, in the time (if we remember aright) of Shaun the Proud, even to the old flag of the O'Neills flying gaily from its high turret. But these are centuries and centuries older. The *Musée Plantin* at Antwerp shows the progress of printing at its infancy. By a happy thought the exhibits are housed in the printer Plantin's ancient *château*, and the furniture and appointments are exactly as he left them when he died in 1589. But then any one of these islets is much more interesting, in as much as it takes us back a thousand years further, back into the very twilight of history. Pompeii was preserved to us by the deluging lava of Vesuvius exactly as it was in the first century, these happily by their inaccessibility. Everything keeps its authentic accent and colour. Time alone, it may be said, has injured their relics; and time had to do with hard granite. The storms sweeping over those exposed bluffs are of course fierce and frequent. But the wildest Atlantic gales and even " the tempest's fiery breath " are more merciful by far than the mainland's devastating human vandalism. The inhabitants were martyred or murdered several times by the Danes (we intend no bull); but what plunder had the pirates to carry away with them where everything bore the impress of Gospel simplicity ? Unlikely that the poor recluses had second tunics. So after a time the Danes passed these islands by. They were hard to climb and not worth sacking after all their trouble. So it happens that we have the past in the present; bits of the sixth in the twentieth century; sixth and seventh century churches and monasteries, minus nonessentials, just as they were away away back in the time of men, many of whom imbibed the spirit of asceticism from St. Patrick's own personal teaching, as he in his turn had learned it in the island of Lerins. In Pompeii you may indeed see the first century. But what a contrast is there not between the revelations of Pompeii and those of Skellig Michael or Inishmurray ? Roman luxury and naked vice in the one, heroic virtue and the simple life at its best in the other For on those lonely ocean rocks lived and died, and are buried beneath the unnamed cross-scribed slabs, that now the grey lichen covers and the mossy sea-pink arises to decorate, the very flowers of the Irish race.

Connemara's Ardoilen is another ancient ecclesiastical museum. Its protection is likewise both its inaccessibility, and—as in the case of the others—the Alpine climb needed to reach its surface. It contains a sixth or early seventh century anchoretical establishment which Petrie regards as perhaps one of the best preserved in Europe. In his monumental work, " The Ecclesiastical Architecture of Ireland Anterior to the Anglo-Norman Invasion,"[1] this distinguished Irish scholar, to whom the country can never be sufficiently grateful, has a long dissertation on this old-world religious home and its various parts. Exact measurements of even every window and doorway are given in feet and inches. He speaks about the monks' little cells, which formed ' the Laura'; the abbot's habitation, more com-

---
[1] p. 419, etc.

modious and loftier, as befitted the island's ruler, "built with much rude art," and having its private passage to the chapel; the refectory, externally round internally square; the gallery, whose use he cannot make out, too large for a store-room, too small for an ambulatory or cloister; the great tomb or sarcophagus, most probably designed for the founder—a St. Fechin—the covering slab carved and one of its sides ornamented with a chiselled human figure; the stone church—everything is, of course, in durable stone— its entrance on the west, its altar still remaining. It is, he states, " among the rudest [and therefore, we may presume, among the oldest] of the ancient edifices, which the fervour of the Christian religion raised on its introduction into Ireland."

All these are situated within a great circular stone wall —technically the cashel—the area so enclosed being 108 feet in diameter. 'The enclosure,' you can see, in olden times had pretty manifest boundaries. Nowadays, though in convents of men or women it has abated none of its importance, as often as not it is, like a parallel of latitude, an imaginary line laid down by the rules.

Outside the enclosure, on both sides of its entrance, are circular buildings. In pre-Patrician times in Ireland, we may remark, any other kind of structure was exceptional. The Irish fashion, though perpetuated in the Round Towers, only gradually lost its vogue. But its presence invariably points to a very hoary age. These buildings Petrie takes to be probably the Guest Houses. That, too, is their location in a present-day monastery. In fact you would almost fancy he is describing, not a pre-mediaeval religious institution, but a modern Cistercian or Benedictine Abbey, so close is the resemblance.[1]

Crosses, crosses, everywhere; inscribed on the church door lintel, embellishing the sides of the sarcophagus, crowning the altars or penitential stations which are the prominent objects in the grounds surrounding the enclosure.

In these grounds, too, there is an artificial lake and a well laid out walk along it. Go down by it for about two hundred yards, down to the sheltered little valley. There

---

[1] The omitted details are very significant for a professed antiquary. But to the general reader they would be of small interest.

you will find standing by itself another comparatively large oval stone house. Not improbably it was the community's Infirmary or Sanatorium. It has its enclosed garden, and its own artificial lakelet. As one may fairly infer, however severe on themselves, they softened the austerities, and gave every care and attention to the sick and infirm, and we may be sure to the very old. Moreover, it has, as you would expect, its own altar, surmounted of course by a cross.

The little necropolis, or city of the dead, is within the cashel or enclosure. As in the case of the Kerry island, described a few pages before this, the individual graves are here also marked—when they are marked—by the same symbol of Christianity; either by simple stone crosses, or else by flagstones " sculptured with rude crosses but without letters." Is it again a seventh century or a twentieth century abbey cemetery that he is talking about ? At all events they are exactly alike. The twentieth century monks and nuns, like their *confrères* of Ardoilen 1,300 years ago, have the same unwritten epitaphs. They ambition no other. And in death as in life, one might almost say, they, too, cling to the sign of redemption. *Deus meus et omnia.*

There is another of these monastic islands that is little talked about, and yet perhaps it is the most typical ocean dysert of them all—Bishop's Island not far from old Kilkee. In late Irish it is called the Island-of-the-starving-Bishop, and a story goes with the name. Nowadays the contracted appellation is generally used. Wakeman, a distinguished antiquary of the modern school, a non-Catholic, of course, as they all are, describes it in his own matter-of-fact style :

> It is, [he says, after remarking that the ancient solitaires appear to have selected the wildest and most dreary spots as their abode], a barren precipitous rock, environed by perpendicular or over-hanging cliffs, about 250 feet in height. It contains about three quarters of an acre of surface, to which access is most difficult, and only to be effected by a skilful climber and after a long continuance of calm weather. . . . Such is the lonely and desolate character of the place, that even the very birds appear in some measure to have lost their instinctive dread of intruders ; and at the time of our visit the ground was literally strewn with their eggs, laid upon a few twigs of heath,

or upon withered grass or straw, which had probably been picked up from the surface of the sea.[1]

In the *Nineteenth Century* (March, 1895) the late Miss Emily Lawless, the Irish poetess,[2] has a beautiful article on St. Fechin of Cluain-Duach in Corca Bascinn (South Clare),[3] the first builder of Round Towers, who died there some time in the eighth century, most likely burned alive by the Danes. In it she charmingly sketches the same islet, putting the words in the mouth of an humble monk, " very unlearned and unskilled in writing," he confesses himself, who as an ' obedience ' has to pen down the life of the saint just mentioned. He is manifestly impressed by above all the embarrassments of approach.

And that western ocean, and portion of that Western Ocean [along Thomond] is known, the old monk writes in his simple archaic style, to be the fiercest and most robustious in the entire world. For the waves of the sea beat eternally against the rocks along its edge, the water rising up, whitely, even to the top of the same, so that in the winter time, or in the great gales of autumn, no man can approach the shore without his soul failing him. .... Now in the midst of this fury of the ocean there are found along that part of the shore of Erinn a great store of islands, which are called of the people *illauns*, *skerries*, or *carrigeens*, according to their size. And against these *illauns*, *skerries*, and *carrigeens* the waves attain to a yet greater violence than elsewhere, they being of such a small size, and having the sea upon every side of them. And several of them bear a very evil and deadly reputation, such as the one called Innis Gloire, upon which no woman, nor yet creature of the sex of woman, dare land but she will immediately die, or yet again another upon

---

[1] " Handbook of Irish Antiquities," 2nd Edition, 1891, p. 148.
[2] She is the author of the pathetic lines descriptive of the Irish soldier—she intended them for ' The Wild Geese ' :—
  " War battered dogs are we,
    Fighters in every clime,
    Fillers of trench and grave,
    Mockers bemocked by time ;

  " War dogs hungry and grey,
    Gnawing a naked bone ;
    Fighting in every clime
    Every cause but our own."
[3] Not to be confounded with St. Fechin of Fore, County Westmeath, of the seventh century, who has been snatched from obscurity, and his life fascinatingly written by Fr. Coyle, C.SS.R. ; nor with their namesake of Ardoilen, who still awaits a biographer ; nor yet with the patron of the diocese of Ross, who is equally ' unhonoured and unsung.'

the which whoso toucheth it, or even toucheth aught that hath grown on it, his flesh and his skin withereth, and the hairs of his head drop off. But of all those islands in the Western Ocean the one which at that time bore the worst and the deadliest reputation was a small and very steep *illaun* lying a little way from off the land, which was known as the Wicked *illaun*, and by no other name [later Bishop's Island], being so called by reason of the curse which St. Enda of Aran had laid upon it. For St. Enda having sent certain of his monks from the three holy islands to visit St. Senan in his monastery at Inis Catargh,[1] on the way back they were caught in a great storm, and the waves rising higher and higher—Satan himself doubtless assisting from beneath—their curraghs were cast ashore and dashed to pieces against the *illaun*, the sides of which were too steep for them to climb.

In the end of his most eventful life, after much travel and many adventures, hither, never heeding St. Enda's curse, the grand old man, St. Fechin, came. "And here he built himself a cell of loose stones, roofing it over with scraws, which he cut from the turf. And there he abode for two years and seven months [*i.e.* until his death or martyrdom by the Danes] even as his namesake, St. Fechin of Conmacne-Mara had abode in a like cell upon the little island of Ard Oilen, . . . living upon shell-fish and stale bread, of which a bag was left at the foot of the cliff, seeking and finding a desert in the ocean (*quaerere desertum in Oceano*) as holy men and confessors of Erinn have in all ages delighted to do."

May he rest in peace.

---

[1] Iniscattery.

Chapter VII

FADED MEMORIES

SHOULD LOCAL SAINTS BE FORGOTTEN ?—SHOULD IRISH MISSIONARY SAINTS ?—ST. GALL—STORY—POEM—NOTE OF APOLOGY.

"Happy is the nation that has a glorious army of Saints! Happy still more if the nation never forgets them!"—Doctor Hedley (Dedication Sermon, St. Brigid's Church, Ardagh.)

IN the discussion of a previous chapter we were labouring to show that it is a sin and a shame that Irish saints should be all forgotten; that Martin of Derry, Saerghus of Cork, Cummian of Tipperary, Aengus the Culdee (*i.e.*, the servant of God—Céile Dé) of Limerick, as well as Diarmad of Castledermot, etc., etc., contrary to what the good English Bishop—the innocent man—a few years ago took for granted, are now at best mere names, *voces et nihil praeterea*; that St. Nuadha (or Nuadhat) of Roscommon no less than Fulterach, St. Fynen, St. Naithfraich and St. Auxil belonging to Kildare are not even that, scarcely an echo [1] of their names lingering in the very districts distinguished as well as blessed and sanctified by their presence, and still undoubtedly enjoying the inheritance of their teaching and religious influence. For men perish, ideas do not. Moreover, now powerful with God, we may be sure that their spirits still hover over the scenes of their earthly pilgrimage, and that they lovingly guard and protect their spiritual descendants. Yet they are themselves ignored and unknown! For the unlettered and hard-working peasant an excuse may be found. But even those of us

---

[1] The part of Roscommon south of the town of Roscommon and Lanesborough and along Lough Ree was in ancient times one of the seven Delvin territories and was called Delvin-Nuadat. This seems like an echo, but it is an echo that has died out.
Hy-Many, the country of the O'Kellys, extended from the Shannon to Galway Bay. It originally included the portion of Roscommon just defined, *i.e.*, Delvin-Nuadat

who have had the very best opportunities for education, and passed examinations without number, may have to make a confession as little to our credit as Montalembert's, though he afterwards amply atoned for it.[1] On leaving college many of us, like him, knew by heart the list of Jupiter's mistresses (and Henry VIII's wives); but as to our country's—not to speak of our county's—saints and scholars and European civilisers, except St. Patrick and maybe St. Columbkille, we never heard there were such.

Very likely you admit it is a pity. But perhaps you respond that these old Irish saints would have it so; that even in their own times they hid away from the world and wished, like Gemma Galgani and Claire Ferchaud of our own days, to be ignored and effaced, the world forgetting by the world forgot; that they lived for God and not for man, except in so far as serving man brought them nearer to God. Quite true. But why extinguish the inspiration of their example? of their simplicity and unselfishness, their learning, their heroic self-conquest? Even a little taper set on one's own table gives one more light than a brilliant lamp burning miles and miles off.

" They that live as models for the mass
　　Are singly of more value than them all.
　Keep but the model safe, new men will rise
　　To prove how great a good that Laura hath but lived."(?)

These lines, imperfectly quoted, make indifferent verse; but all the same they contain sound sense. Kildare, for instance, has had through the centuries many illustrious men; but none really greater than those who of old settled down in its solitudes, and figuratively, and in many cases quite literally, made these " dyserts " bloom like gardens. Kildare is the poorer for forgetting and losing them. Kildare is by so much less likely to reproduce good and great men for thoughtlessly shattering its humanly perfect models. And this is equally true of every county in Ireland.

Precisely like Moone, St. Gall is the title both of a town and a canton in Switzerland; but of a great town, not of a wayside village, and of a full canton, which is an independent state, not of a scrap of a county. But it imports

---

[1] " Monks of the West," Vol. I., Introduction, chapter ii.

more. Town and canton have not squeezed out of existence, as frogs are said to, the parent from which they sprung. St. Gall's monastery is still there, and still flourishing; amongst other things one of the richest repositories of Irish MSS. and Irish literature on the continent of Europe. Yet it was established away back at the beginning of the seventh century, fully 700 years before the forgotten Franciscans recited their first Matins in Moone. Its foundations were laid in what was then a swampy 'dysert,' not unlike our Corcach-more or Fasagh Luiminagh, and by an Irishman. For St. Gall was an Irishman; and a patriotic one, too, as his strenuous battle for Irish customs proves. His name is, of course, not mentioned once in a blue moon amongst us, outside of the Marist and the Christian Brothers' schools, and these institutions must always be honourably excepted. But that's our way. We are no better in Kerry or Derry, it has to be confessed, than they are in Kildare or Roscommon. We could hardly be much worse than them. That's one consolation anyway.

A more solid consolation is that, though unknown with us, they are not unhonoured everywhere. "The people of Cornwall," writes the English Camden who died in 1623, "have always borne such veneration to Irish saints, who retired there, that almost all their towns have been consecrated to their memory." The Cornish are Kelts. So they went among their own, and their own received them. But they went further. The north of England the Irish monks of Lindisfarne, off the coast of Northumberland, evangelised and civilised. Their influence, like the sunshine, was felt everywhere throughout England. The history of Glastonbury, in Somerset, goes back before the age of written records. It is Tennyson's island-valley of Avilion.

"During the Saxon period, it increased in renown and influence; it became indeed the centre of Christianity in southern and western England. Although we have little proof of the fact," continues Cardinal Gasquet, "it seems almost certain that wandering Irish scholars came over to Glastonbury, tarried and taught there for a while, and departing left behind them their books and treatises to be the treasured possessions of future generations of scholars."[1]

"The Greater Abbeys of England," p. 103.

Again they went further; for, as the brilliant Frenchman already referred to, Count de Montalembert, testifies, in the 7th and 8th centuries the monastic nation became *par excellence* the missionary nation.

Scores of Irish saints, like St. Gall, are reverenced as the patron saints of Continental churches and dioceses from Antwerp to Marseilles; and commemorated, too, by the popular local Kermesse, those joyous parish holidays of eight days, which correspond to the church octave and follow the celebration of the patron saints' anniversaries. In Fr. Treacy's stanzas, given at the end of this chapter, will be found the names of many of them, more briefly, simply, and beautifully put than any one could hope to do it. But these men are, like the prophets, without honour in their own country—individually quite unknown.

Yet they reflect the greatest honour upon it. That you must admit whatever your point of view. If you are unappreciative of unselfishness and transparent sincerity, then you must admire their blameless lives; if sanctity and an evangelising spirit make no strong appeal to you, then remember that such men were, generally speaking, men of the loftiest eloquence, the most profound knowledge, the most indomitable wills, and the most forceful character. By any standard by which even the world weighs men they were among the world's greatest.

True, a thorough "man of affairs" of this twentieth century, even he with a veneer of religion for respectability and Sundays, is not unapt in his own mind to pronounce them patent fools. Their ideals are meaningless to him, and he cannot understand them.[1] But, on the other hand, they would unhesitatingly declare him exactly the same, though according to their wont they would employ a much gentler phrase. And they were as clear-sighted as he, as learned and as wise as he, and they knew men and things quite as well as he, let him be whoever he may. Which is right? Let us leave it an open question. Its discussion otherwise would take us wrangling back to bedrock axioms, and be as long as he considered last Sunday's sermon. But let the man-of-affairs with his weekly church-going recognise at all events, that he has no right nor tittle of title to set

---

[1] V. I. Cor. ii. 14.

himself up in the controversy as Judge and Jury. Surely, as a sensible man-of-the-world, he would not dream of doing that. There are things undreamt of in his philosophy. A mathematician generally makes a poor linguist, and a good linguist an indifferent astronomer.

This is not a spiritual manual. All that is being insisted on is the existence in these saints of the very qualities that the world most highly esteems, and to honour those distinguished by them, when they are gone it raises in its great cities statues and monuments: ability and genius, perfect command of themselves, sincerity, fearlessness even unto death in doing what they believed to be the right, anxiety and success in helping others and in spreading the blessings of ciivlisation. Providence no doubt moulded them for the work for which they were specially intended. It pleased God " to fill them with the spirit of understanding, and they poured forth the words of His wisdom as showers," and " He directed their counsel, and their knowledge." Nevertheless they show the stock from which they sprung, the missionary race issuing from an island home and passing " into strange countries," which was and is and, we hope, is to be, and shining once more with renewed brilliancy in far Eastern climes. Politically Ireland may be unenvied and unenviable, the Niobe among nations, an Israel in bondage weeping by the waters of Babylon; yet religiously to make up for it, possibly to some extent because of it, she is the Queen of all of them. Catholic Belgium, Germany, France, and Switzerland have taken her heroic spiritual sons to themselves as their very own; Catholic Ireland, with a spendthrift's prodigality, has to its shame cast out their very names. A story, if rather long, may illustrate this. It may perhaps, too, afford evidence of a kind that in their regard, despite the shortcomings of their own, the saying of Ecclesiasticus is verified: " The memory of him shall not depart away, and his name shall be in request from generation to generation." [1]

About a score of years ago Fr. John Walsh built a new church near the Chippewa Indians in Minnesota, in a new parish that had been cut out for him by his Bishop, Dr.

---

[1] xxxix. 13.

McGolrick, who was the first Bishop of Duluth ; a diocese which had been established for him in his turn a few years before, (1889) just in the same way but by the Pope himself ; and has already, according to the latest available statistics, about a hundred churches, and dear knows how many schools and convents.

Both the names and the facts crushed and crowded anyhow into this sagging sentence will tell their own tale of Irish Missionary zeal in the United States, if only you have time to take them out, one by one, and examine them.

Anyway Fr. Walsh built his church and put a steeple to it. But then a schism broke out in the new parish and the Arian schism was nothing to it. His parishioners, fresh arrivals all in these parts like himself, were half Irish and half German. It was coming on to the great day of the Bishop's arrival and of the consecration or solemn blessing when, as everybody knows, a church has formally and for life to get the name of a saint or something, just as a new-born infant has at baptism.[1] The Germans said it would be but right that the saint should be a German saint. Then the Irish got their backs up and would have no one but an Irish saint. Feelings rose to Sinn Fein election pitch. The honour of ' Fatherland ' and of ' Motherland ' was at stake, and neither party would budge an inch. Compromise was scouted by the belligerents : like our peace talk of some years ago, it was nothing but subtle enemy manoeuvring. Poor Fr. Walsh was at his wits' end, and did not know what the dickens to do.

At long last a bright thought struck him, and he proposed they would cast lots for it. This they all agreed to. It was arranged that five Germans and five Irishmen would meet him in the sacristy on the following Sunday at a Peace Conference and draw lots ; the winners on the spot to declare the name of the saint of their choice, and all there and then to bury the hatchet and have done with it. " It's as fair as fair could be," they all chorused.

On that Sunday evening after all was over Fr. Dan. Lynch, the Assistant Priest, was sauntering down to the

---

[1] The right time for selecting the Patron of a church or rather the Titular is before the foundation stone is laid. But Fr. Walsh was so busy collecting, he never thought of it.

church, and whom did he meet but big Pat. Moran, one of the plenipotentiaries. Pat. was looking very glum.

"Well, Pat." said he, "and how did you do?"

"Rotten bad, yir Reverence, rotten bad."

"What! did ye lose it?"

"Indeed and we did, yir Reverence," Pat. replied, "the Dutchies has it. But I wouldn't mind that so much, but the way Fr. Walsh carried on. You wouldn't believe it."

"Why, what did he do?" inquired Fr. Lynch.

"Well then, I'd be ashamed to tell yir Reverence. But when the Dutchies won, and up and told him the name of their oul' saint, he laughed and he laughed, you'd think some one had presented him with a marble altar; an' us thinkin' all the time he was on our side. I'll never, no never the longest day I live——"

"And did he say nothing?" interposed Fr. Lynch.

"How could he, man," answered Pat. angrily, "and him a-chokin'? I'd be ashamed of me life if any Prodestan' seen a priest laughin' like yon. There they wor, the Dutchies and our own priest gigglin' and sniggerin' and crowin' over it in our faces, and him the worst out. As long as I——"

"But what anyway did they call it?" again interjected Fr. Lynch.

"What did they call it, is it? Well, as well as I mind, I think it was Saint Killian or somethin'. But, yir Reverence, I'll never——"

"My great goodness!" exclaimed Fr. Lynch. "Sure Killian is an Irish saint."

"An Irish saint!" echoed Pat. and he jumped almost two feet off the ground, "Killian an Irish saint!" he repeated. "Don't be talkin', Father Dan."

"Aye is he," continued Fr. Lynch, "born in Ireland, and what's more in my own parish of Mullagh, County Cavan, at home. He went off with himself, of course, in old times like another, so he did, to convert the Belgians or Dutchies or some of them. But Irish he is, as Irish as Tara Hill."

"Well, Fr. Dan, but that bangs Banagher," was all poor Pat. could say. He was quite dumbfounded and did not know whether he was standing on his head or his heels. But the blank glumness had given way to a sunny smile.

"Beggin' yir Reverence's pardon, Father Dan, yir

Reverence, if you plaze," he said, " I must be off to tell the neighbours."

The Monks of Erin

The Irish Monks, the Irish Monks,
   Their names are treasured still,
In many a foreign valley,
   And many a foreign hill.
Their preaching, prayers and fasting
   Are still the peasants' themes,
Around the coast of Cornwall
   And along old Flanders' streams.
Their lives, austere and holy,
   And the wonder of their hands,
Still nourish faith and sanctity
   Through fair Italia's lands.
The cross they bore in triumph
   Oh ! bright as ever shines
Above the domes of Austria,
   Among the Tuscan vines.

Sedulius, the poet,[1]
   And Columbkille, the dove,
At Rome and Hy are honoured
   And remembered still with love.
At Lucca St. Frigidian,[2]

---

[1] He is entitled " the Virgil of Sacred Poetry." The influence of the recently converted Irish on the Continent began with his works, which were published in the fifth century. So we can see how appropriate it is that he should be mentioned first. His *Carmen Paschale* is the first great Christian epic worthy of the name, states Dr. Sigerson. Parts of it have been hallowed by their universal use throughout the Church. Lines in it to the B.V.M. are often quoted. They begin in a translation :—
" Safe from the rugged thorn springs up the tender rose,
   In honour hides the parent stem, in beauty's softness grows ;
So from the sinful stem of Eve all-sinless Mary came
   To cover and to expiate her mother's deed of shame."
According to Hyde, Sedulius, the poet, finally made Achaia in Greece his home. There are, he adds, at least eight noted saintly Irishmen of that name (=, in English, Shiel) commemorated by Colgan.
Another of them was Abbot of Kildare in the eighth century. " He won," says Cardinal Moran, " a distinguished fame by his commentaries on the Gospels and the Pauline Epistles . . . . and was the illustrious ornament of the Church of Kildare."—*V.* Dr. Moran's " Essays on the Early Irish Church," pp. 236–7.
Columbkille, the writer found better known about Inverness than anywhere in Ireland.

[2] *Alias* Finnian (+576). A prince of Ultonia he was educated at Rome. He founded, about 540, the celebrated School of Moville at the head of Strangford Lough. Afterwards returning to Italy he became Bishop of Lucca. (*V.* his Office, March 22nd). Not to be confounded with St. Finnian, " the Guide of the Saints of Ireland," and founder of Clonard in Meath, who died about the year 552.

DYSERT DIARMADA

In a church ablaze with lights,
Is honoured with pure worship,
'Mid the pomp of Roman rites.
Even still the British miners
Exult on Piaran's [1] feast,
And though they hate the Church of Rome,
They venerate her priest.
The bells of sweet Tarentum,
As they wake the matin air,
Still tell in tones of gladness,
That Cataldus's [2] faith is there.

Queen Mechlin's noble temple
To an Irish monk is raised,
In every home in Mechlin
St. Romuald's name is praised.
Virgilius, the gifted, [3]
In his glorious Salzburg tomb
Is honoured by the silent prayer
And by the cannon's boom.
Old hymns are sung to Fridolin, [4]
In the islands of the Rhine,
And the relics of Besancon's saint
Sleep in a silver shrine.

---

[1] St. Ciaran. With our cousins the Welsh Celts, the letter " p " was a favourite, to the old Irish it was taboo. These characteristic peculiarities should not be overlooked by students of the antiquity of Keltic. They are fully gone into in the first chapter of Douglas Hyde's " Literary History of Ireland."
English-speaking westerns are yet unsafe in the use of the letter ' p.' In Mayo and Galway schools, a National School Inspector informs us, one of the commonest mistakes is the use of ' b ' for ' p.' Com*b*osed they will write and not com*p*osed, the *b*ragmatical jackdaw and not the *p*ragmatical, and their orthography reflects their orthoepy. In the light of Hyde's discussion this unreliability is quite interesting. Besides this Apostle there were several saints of the name.

[2] Cathal or Cathaldus, a native of Momonia, flourished in the beginning of the seventh century, San Cataldo, a town in the heel of Italy near Taranto, still bears his name. Before leaving Ireland he was lecturer in the great College, or rather in the pre-mediaeval University of Lismore, which had just been founded by St. Carthach (*alias* Carthage), about 632. Lismore, like Clonmacnoise, Bangor, Armagh, etc., was frequented in crowds by Anglo-Saxon, Gaulish, Teuton, Swiss, and Italian students in those days. As many as 3,000 of them from all parts of Europe are said to have been together at Armagh.
In 1173 Strongbow was bought off from burning Lismore. In spite of this his son plundered it the very next year—not a bad instance of what is termed *Punica fides*. Four years later the English again sacked it and destroyed it as ruthlessly and thoroughly as the Germans did Louvain. To-day of its schools and cloisters and its twenty churches there is not a stone upon a stone.

[3] Called in the ancient Annals Ferghil the Geometer. He was perhaps the most learned mathematician and astronomer, as well as one of the greatest saints, of the eighth century.

[4] Surnamed " the traveller." He evangelised Thuringia in Germany and was appointed Bishop by Pope Zachary in 741.

FADED MEMORIES

The voice that roused Crusaders
By the Tagus, Rhone, and Po,
Seems ringing still o'er Malachy
At the convent of Clairvaux.

The Irish Monks, the Irish Monks,
Their spirit [1] still survives
In the stainless Church of Ireland,
As in her priesthood's lives.
Their spirit still doth linger
'Round Holycross and Kells,
Oh! Ireland's monks can know no death
While gush our holy wells.[2]
High Cashel's fane is standing,
And, though in the spoiler's hand,
Like the captive ark of Juda,
'Tis a blessing to our land;
For proudly it reminds us
Of the palmy days of yore,
When Kings were Monks, and Monks were Kings,
Upon our Irish shore.

William J. Treacy, S.J.

A Note of Apology

The manner in which, during the early centuries, Ireland's sons Christianised both Scotland and England and carried the lamp of civilisation to even the furthermost corners of Europe, is a superb subject for minute investigation. It hardly concerns us here except indirectly. In touching upon it we have dealt with it in a fashion so necessarily meagre and unsatisfactory that it must be vexatious to both the well read and to the genuine student. It looks not unlike ' damning with faint praise.' It may go some way towards making amends if we supplement and confirm the few details given by a quotation from an exceptionally well informed article, on the same theme, which appeared recently, as a sub-leader in a Dublin daily paper. Necessarily it, too, barely brushes the fringe of the subject.

The article begins and ends with applications to current politics. These we omit.

. . . . . The missionary expansion of
Ireland, which had begun before Colmcille,

---

[1] This is the very utmost he could say, poet and all as he is.
[2] ?

put forth its rich blossoms with the apostolate of that great saint of the Irish Church to Scotland. From Scotland his followers spread over Northern England, and continued their labours in Wales and the South until in the seventh century missionary routes were traced across Great Britain by the footprints of the Irish saints on their way to the Continent, in addition to those who made the voyage direct from Ireland to the Armorican coast, Brendan and other voyaging saints had evangelised Iceland before its discovery by the Norwegians, and had won to Christianity the northern isles. The rich fruits were garnered by Saint Columbanus and Saint Gall, and their work was maintained and extended by the host of minor pilgrims that followed in their wake, founding schools, monasteries and abbeys from the Appenines to the North Sea, from the Bay of Biscay to the very east of Europe. The most notable battlefields in the late war bear the names of these early civilisers of Europe. Saint Gobain Wood, the key to the military situation in France, is called after the Irish saint of that name, who established his school and monastery there. The diocese of Saint Dié on the eastern frontier, the dioceses of Verdun, Malines, Gand were founded by missionary saints from Ireland. In Peronna Scottoran is the tomb of Saint Fursey. Reims, Laon, Cambrai, and Meaux, Chateau Thierry and other towns on the Marne were centres of Irish scholastic foundations, constantly staffed with monks from Ireland, whither princes, prelates and scholars of the Continent come for instruction.

In the tenth and eleventh century the wave of Irish culture spread through Germany, in whose universities of to-day are found the vellums, classics glossed with Gaelic, from which the schoolmaster-monk from Ireland taught. Nor did Irish expansion stop here. It followed the course of the Danube to the confines of the Black Sea. At the end of the eleventh century, we know from a letter to the king of Bohemia, Vratislav, of a mission to Poland, and from the records preserved in the Academy of Science at Cracow that the Irish monks reached Kiev, the capital of the

Ukraine, and this "Misya Irlandska" is described as the origin of Christianity in Poland and Southern Russia. This great missionary and civilising movement which moved forward, in the face of the advancing hordes from the East, Christianising and civilising them as they met, was continued until the landing of the English in Ireland in the twelfth century. Almost the first act of the invaders was the burning of the Bachall Iosa, the crozier of Saint Patrick. Their next was to extinguish "the bright lamp which shone on Kildare's holy fane," surely a presage of the dark days that the invasion were to bring upon Ireland and upon Europe. . . . . .

—(*Freeman's Journal*, April 8th, 1919)

Chapter VIII

THE IRISH LAY BROTHER

KELTIC SAINTS IGNORED AT BAPTISM—HIGH-SOUNDING CHRISTIAN(?) NAMES SUBSTITUTED—PICTURES OF IRISH SAINTS UNOBTAINABLE—EGYPTO-IRISH RELIGIOUS.

> "For, if we should be so assiduous in honouring the palms won by foreigners, the crowns gained by strangers, and the triumphs of men who dwelt beyond the sea, so as to make our own what belongs to other regions, how much the more does it not befit us to burn with zeal and to be full of ardour in celebrating the feasts of those who are entitled to devotion from the faithful, to honour from the Church, and to love from their country."
> —From Fourth Lesson of Feasts of All the Saints of Ireland, November 6th.

THE only person the writer ever knew of that paid proper respect to the old Irish Saints was a poor lay brother in a Religious House away down in the west of Ireland. We must tell about him, no matter what happens. He deserves it.

He had charge of the church and baptistery, and his glory in life was to keep them shining and sparkling like diamonds. He was intensely Irish; and, as everybody knows, love of country comes next to love of God. When a baby came to be baptised:

"A lovely little angel, God bless it," he would say, "that you are bringing us. And of all days of the year on St. Ultan's day," if it happened to be that. He had an Irish Saint for almost every day of the year. Then he would begin about St. Ultan. We are afraid that sometimes, before he stopped, the patience of those who were not quite so enthusiastic about Gaelic Saints, and who were anxious that the baby would be home again soon, and catch no cold, was severely tried. But everybody liked him. "He talks," they said, "like a prayer book," and they would bear with anything sooner than annoy him, or not appear interested.

"And what are we going to call it?" was the first question. If it was Michael or Jeremiah or Josue or even

Desmond, he shrugged his shoulders but said nothing. If it was, let us say, Laserian or Brendan or Kevin, he was in ecstacies. He just ran off and had Father Cyril, or Father Oswald, or whoever was in charge for the week, at the font while you'd be saying trapsticks. If Alexander or Albert or Hubert, or anything new and ' swanky,' then there was a tussle. Should all his entreaties prove of no avail, and they declined point blank to call " the little angel " even by the name " it brought with it," you would pity him to see him for a week afterwards. Indeed, on the last occasion he was there, when a young heir was brought to this semi-parochial church and was called George, " after his grandfather," there were ructions. He lost his temper, poor fellow—the only occasion on which it was ever known to happen—and gave out not quite too complimentary things about grandfathers who maybe weren't in heaven at all, and oul' British Kings who certainly weren't.

But it was taken out of him. We must go into that fully. Then you will see for yourself how venially venial was his fault. St. Francis de Sales at his best could not stand what he stood.

There was a certain Mrs. Gamplet who was by long chalks the champion *ignoramus*, man or woman, of the seven parishes, at least in matters aesthetical and theological. She was convoying the party. To do honour to her most respectable client's little occasion, she was arrayed in her full-dress regimentals : her green go-to-meetings skirt, her red bonnet with blue ribbons and heliotrope roses jostling one another all over it, every one of them the size of a small pancake. Her cheeks, too, that day were also a bit heliotrope, and her eyes were sparkling and twinkling beneath the red bonnet like the burnished brass knobs of the lay Brother's candle-sticks. She was on her mettle, too. Her dignity and authority, she considered, were questioned by any interference. That, above all before others, she could not brook. Unlettered and all as she was, she was top match for the simple Brother with the tongue ; or, for that matter, for anybody else.

" I've got me strict conjunctions," said she, " and I'll not depart from them for any lame man if he's a priesht itself." And then, " Mind your own busyness, me day-sint man, and I'll mine mine. What's that to you if we called 'im Wallaby-Day-Broke ? " [1]

And then, at intervals, as " rechalleys," and as the spirit moved her, to the young sponsors and a few others standing by. They were looking daggers at her all the time, but she never noticed it. Only a strong leather muzzle, with straps to it, could hold her anyway.

" The oul' fool! You'd think with his airs he could baptise a chile himself. But sure they say—though I nivir let on or spake a word about it meself, bekeys I wouldn't—they say, so they do, that even Father Wulstan, the Prire, couldn't baptise a christian in this—what do you call it? Aye, scullery, in this scullery, ony the circular clargy lets them." . . .

" Me head is splittin' open with his saints and his saints every time I come here. He's ivir and always at it, ding-dong. Why doesn't he stop some time, and go and say his prayers ? " . . . .

" It's a spite he has agin me, so it is, good and all as he purtends for to be. I'll tache him." . . .

" Heigh-ho! you'd think he was Prire of the parish or somebody, so you would, the way he gits on. He lets nobody have a say in anything ony himself. But wait to I see Father Isidore." . . .

And then as a parting shot, and though fired, we believe, at random, it was the one shot that told and ruffled the poor lay Brother's temper :

" The oul' nidderin' fool! It's a world's wonder to me he didn't give himself a day-sint Irish-spoken name, he's so purticlar, whin he was at it. But it's the likes o' thim that's nivir done talkin'. It's not do as I do, but do as I say, for me and me else, with 'im anyway."

A bright young student home on his holidays from St. Jarlath's or Mungaret's—we don't know which—who was coming out after doing his hour or something, stopped at the notices, making out he was reading them, and overheard all from the baptistery. It was a good long way in off the church, a temporary arrangement, but the door was wide open. He gives graphic details of the battle of the names,

---

[1] Not a bad drive at a very aristocratic and high-sounding name, Willoughby de Broke.

and as he is a perfect mimic you would swear you were just listening to her. He had them in roars in the corridor one wet Sunday evening after he went back. He says the Blazer was in her best form. The Northern Blazer, by the way, was her nickname, or, as we should style it in writing, her *sobriquet*. Behind her back—never, you may be sure, before her face—everyone called her that. Nobody would know whom you were talking about if you said Mrs. Gamplet. The Brother kept on very modestly but firmly expostulating, he says. But she—

"It's a mortial sin," she snapped at the first going off, "for to go to say there is no St. Garge. Bekeys there is." . .

"No, I didn't read it in your oul' books. Why should I ? Bekeys what's in print is all lies and make-ups, the half of it. Ivirybody what reads the papers knows that. But I seen him in a holy picture. It was blessed too, so it was, by Father Sicklebirth [Sigebert ?] at the last Mission, who's a walkin' saint this day, and has no fagaries like half the people that's goin'." . . .

"You needn't be talkin'. Saint Garge is a grander saint nor Saint Columbus [Columba ?]. Aye is he, any day he rises, for all your book larnin'. Didn't he kill the divil with a prod of his swoord or somethin', didn't he ? Answer me that. And that's what Saint Columbus nivir done. More betoken, haven't I the poto of thim murderin' other in me own parlour at home ? And grand he lucks ridin' his white horse and the divil squallin' under him. An' the divil scure to 'im ! An' still and with all you'll go and trape on a body he was ony a Dunaun or a mite or what-somedever you call it."

The St. Jarlath man avers that the Blazer wound up by calling the Brother " an Egypshun hero-glib-tick " [hieroglyphic ?] and a " two footed hippo-possumus." There is a sting for him in these titles certainly; but they are far beyond her, clever as she is. We don't believe a word of it. Students are noted rascals for adding fringes and flounces to the plain truth.

Anyway, is it any wonder that flesh and blood couldn't stand her any longer ? Still, be it recorded to his credit, he never once threw the offensive '*sobriquet*' at her, although he knew it perfectly well; and knew, too, that a whisper of it would floor her. He had that much restraint over himself at the worst of times. Had he, though, the war of Troy would have been nothing to it.

Nine or ten days after this, the Superior-General, the Very Reverend Father Ildephonsus, promoted the lay Brother to his own magnificent church—and no baptistery.

> You keep everything so immaculate and beautiful, Dear Brother, he wrote, that you are only lost down there. We desire to have you near ourselves. Work and merit always deserve recognition.
> We have heard, Dear Brother, with deep interest of what you so happily term your 'Irish specific'[1] for burnishing, and that you have no use for these foreign, labour-saving compounds so many of which are now on the market. We highly approve of your patent. Results show that, in your case at least, it is the better: it has always been a pleasure to us to enter your charmingly kept edifice. My own observation also tends to confirm your matured opinion that the others, so temptingly advertised, partake, to a not unsubstantial extent, of the nature of frauds. Besides they are so expensive.
> We are highly gratified we assure you, Dear Brother, by your unvaried devotion to whatever duties we felt called upon to assign to you from time to time. As we are thoroughly convinced that you are actuated by the highest motives, we are happy to say that we have not the least fear or misgiving but it will continue unabated in the least. It seems providential, and we are very pleased to be able to inform you of it, that in your new sphere you will have the same congenial task, viz., looking after the House of God, and that already, for this country, a beautiful one; nay, if the new repairs were completed, we might venture to say, almost a perfect one. We can also congratulate ourselves on the great edification your presence is sure to afford to the faithful about us.
>
> Praying, etc., etc.

The poor fellow's heart was stuck in his own church. Every tile of it he had washed, every brass of it he had polished a thousand times over. Had the Superior just written bluntly and briefly—" Clear out of there and report

---

[1] "My patent for cleaning and shining is an Irish one," he used to reply. "It's elbow grease." The dignified Fr. Ildephonsus might obscurely refer to it, but never could he be brought to use an expression so smacking of the commonplace; not if you handed him a fifty-pound note for his new St. Sebastian's altar.

yourself here at 5 *p.m.* to-morrow," he would have obeyed on the spot as a matter of course, without question or demur; and have torn up by the roots out of his heart this sole earthly attachment of his as a temptation of the devil, even though he might tear away a bit of the heart along with it. But after such a nice letter—such a sweet letter—such a long letter—to him a mere lay Brother—to him the most worthless of all the Brothers (as he genuinely believed himself to be)—and from the Superior General himself—from the great Father Ildephonsus himself—every word of it in his own hand-writing, and none of your signed or type-written things!—why, he'd cut his stick for Jamaica with a heart and a half were it only to please him. The good Brother never dreamt of an *arrière pensée*, and never knew of it till his dying day.

God bless Fr. Ildephonsus for treating his humblest-placed subjects with such consideration! But for his name we would certainly say he is a saint. God bless all such thoughtful Superiors! In humbling themselves—if humbling it be—they exalt themselves.

For all that, we wish to goodness that the Superior-General were not half as wise as he is, and had let the poor fellow alone.

The "nice" letter the Brother kept in his big *Key of Heaven*, his only safe, till the day he died. That's how we have come by it. There he had it along with his picture of St. Patrick in green and gold; the one in which our National Apostle holds a solid gold crozier in his left hand, and a Missal or something, bound in superb twentieth century fashion, in his right; his cope flashing a green that takes the sight out of one's eyes; a green so green that, like the gorgeous oleograph adorning the Study Hall of the Irish College, Paris, the shamrocks with which it is plentifully bespangled have to be black or magenta to be seen at all. He had ransacked Dublin for five years, and that was the only prayer-book picture of an Irish saint he could manage to get up to. Often and often he was told most affably and regretfully, " So sorry! But we are just out of them—there's such a run on them," or, " The Irish Saints are just ordered, and will be coming home to us next week. Won't you kindly call again ? " So, despite all his simplicity, it began at last to dawn upon him what these phrases really meant. He never asked for an Irish saint again; and, poor fellow, he did several severe fastings for being the cause of other people's sins. " Thank the Lord," he said, " I am out of such a wicked world." Many a time in the stationery shops was he tempted to buy a French or a German exquisitely dainty, little laced religious picture—photographs some of them from magnificent oil paintings of their country's honoured spiritual heroes, which hang in foreign National Galleries. They looked beautiful. But he resisted the temptation like a man.

" They are only for children," he replied. " Yes, indeed, children will be simply delighted with them," they courteously and cleverly assented. But it was no use.

He was too conscientious in his own way. " They are bad for children," he said to himself. Comparatively not as good as the pictures of Irishmen is, of course, what he meant to say. " There was my pious old aunt at home, may she rest in peace!" he continued to muse, " and I remember well, she taught me far more prayers than ever Father Devine himself, our parish priest; not but he was as good as gold, and what's more a Canon. But he lived three-fourths of his time up in heaven, so he did, and was like nobody. So by these terrible grand saints of other lands. But the little children, God bless them! when they know St. Ailbe and St. Colman and them, then they will know that they, too, by the help of God's grace, can become grand saints themselves some day. Aye can they, just as well as the people at home before them did, if only they like."

As to the baby that, poor innocent! caused all the trouble, you will be pleased to hear that it was never called George after all. A fortnight later it got very sick—stitches was Mrs. Gamplet's diagnosis—and the mother then heard for the first time about the row. She was indignant. She vowed that if it lived she would never call it anything but Aidan, " as that dear saint of a lay Brother, heaven protect him wherever he's gone to! wanted it. No, never."

" It's just the right thing to do, Ma'am," Mrs. Gamplet chimed in. " An' do you know ? it's a far purtier name than Garge any day. An' troth it becomes 'im like a glove. No wonder tha' that nice Brother called it a wee angel.

An' I ever and always liked 'im, so I did, though we had our little differences off and on, an' no harm done. Bekeys he was genewin." " Plaze the Lord," she added, " it'll not die with uz this time, for I'll do me endeyvor. It was the oul' divil himself, and nobody else, that timpted uz to hould out so strong for Garge, or to think of it a tall."

This good lady continued in attendance on such little festive occasions as long as there was a ghost of an excuse, and like a sensible woman she agreed with her patrons in everything. Fadladeen, Grand Nizar and Chamberlain to Aurungzebe, in " Lalla Rookh," could recant his opinions, if they were found displeasing to his Royal Master, while you would be looking about you. But you need not think that this convenient ability is the exclusive privilege of courtiers.

" I'll whip him round the morrow mornin' bright and early," she whispered, " saycretly, under me cloak, to Father Leander. He's a raāl day-sint soort, so he is ; and mebbe he'll stritch a pint—he's furrin you know—an' christen him over agin."

But the mother was shocked ; and no wonder.

" No," she replied firmly, " No, Mrs. Gamplet. No, no, dear. No matter what he's christened, Aidan he is and Aidan he'll be. And, if it pleases the Lord, he will live to be confirmed Aidan."

But she made up her mind, then and there, that she would not assure Mrs. Gamplet she was perfectly well for a further week. It meant little fees, of course—and ' forby.' But no matter.

The baby was all right in ten minutes. Mrs. Gamplet chirruped " Aidan, Aidan " at him morning noon and night, twenty times a minute. She proclaimed—not to say swore— that he knew his name " as well for life as if he was man able." " Luck at him now, the thief of the world ! He opens his little weeshy pearls of eyes every time, and tries his best for to answer me, the darlint ! " She might have hung on for another fortnight, she made herself so useful and agreeable, but for—an urgent call elsewhere. But, wise enough, she left her red bonnet behind her. She had deep reasons of state, best known to herself, for the man- œuvre—the astute reader need not be told what she was up to ;—but she camouflaged them splendidly.

"Pooh!" she exclaimed, "cock them up goin' to thim in me Sunday bonnet. Me dollied cap is good enough for the likes o' thim. An', whisper. They're no way ginteel like others of me customers, I may as well tell you " . . . .

"Oh, no, no, ma'am. For the love of God! Not for a king's hansom in bank money!" . . . .

"Well yes, then, yes. The *deoc an doruis* ov coorse. But let it be small. I'd rather throw it over me left showlder meself, so I would. But sure a body must stick to oul' customs. Why not? Sure there's them what says it's unlucky to . . . ."

And here she began a long rigmarole of a story, the moral in view being that it was the sudden bethinking of the dire and dreadful calamities that follow breaking with old customs that caused her right-about-face. She was politely stopped by forcing on her a second wee *deoc an doruis.* "Just a weeshy wee one, dear. It's the best." She did not throw it over her shoulder, left or right, either.

"Oh, thank you, ma'am, thank you ma'am, it's too good you are, so it is," she kept exclaiming as she pinned a dazzling rainbow shawl beneath her triple chin. " But mind me wee Aidan. For fear of the stitches. He's a love." And off she sailed in her dollied cap.

Fair weather after her!

"Aidan," however, lived to be confirmed Aidan; thanks mainly to Mrs. Gamplet's sudden call. Another day of her " sluthering " and he was gone, if he was the only child in Ireland. Aidan he is to the present day. He is now " man able " and doing well.

Brother Antony was the lay Brother's own name. We should have told you that before, but we didn't like. It has to come out now at last. It was the one cross of his life. "Certainly," he once confided to a lay visitor, " I would love to be called Felim, or Molaise, or anything Irish. Why not? Not but that Saint Antony is one of the greatest saints going."

" No," he replied, " I don't blame the Superiors; because why, that wouldn't be right. They're good men; no better. But they're not infallible. Because why, nobody but the Pope's that. And sure," he continued, " they can't help being toney. Because why, that's the way they're brought up. It's bred in their bones, so it is, Sir this-body's son and Doctor that-body's, and converts the half of them. But we haven't an Irish saint in the house. They're out in the cold, God help them!"

The visitor, it is hardly necessary to state explicitly, was not himself a model of all the virtues; nor was his temper quite so well under control as the good Brother's. He was fuming at what Brother Antony innocently had let drop. For didn't he write his own name and address his letters in Irish characters (the utmost he could do)? As the Blazer would say, "It's the likes o' them that's ever and always the worst." And hadn't he made several eloquent speeches about Irish Ireland off a public platform, hadn't he? and the cheers were still ringing in his ears. But just then Father Casimir, the guest-master, arrived on the scene; and after all he found him as plain and simple and sensible as if he were the Duke of Norfolk's first cousin, or even an Irish peasant. He had indeed a great mind to ask him, as quietly as ever he could manage it, why in the world is it that, above all, the Religious Orders in this country go off to Poland and Spain, and Flanders and Egypt, for their names; and ignore the equally great or greater Irish saints and the second Thebäid, as Father Rushe, a religious himself, happily terms pre-Danish Ireland. But Father Casimir's gentleness and affability almost disarmed him. Besides, he saw he was no match for him. "Maybe it's the best of my play," said he to himself on second thought. "If I but open my mouth I am in for it. He will so overwhelm me with reasons, national and international, that I'm afraid of my life he'll convince me against my will." No reasoning or parleying, but a good, sound—well, a particularly high verbal explosive like a T.T.L. would have relieved his feelings. But in a monastery! Why the towers would crash down as if struck by lightning, aghast at the unheard-of profanity, and bury him alive!—at least the inmates would be astonished if they did not. So what he did was, he did nothing; which was perhaps the best thing to do under the circumstances.

Brother Antony, anyway—in his new home they used to call him Brother Tony; whether as a sly joke, or as an attempt to save his feelings, or simply from affection, was never accurately determined—Brother Antony knew and loved every one of the Irish saints, because they were Irish. He treasured up every scrap of information he could lay hold of about them. His memory for their dates, miracles, and spiritual maxims, grew to be almost as tenacious as that of the Drumcondra Blind Asylum inmate with the phenomenal memory.[1] He made a Litany of their names. Every night after the ordinary prescribed prayers—which were in all conscience long enough—he always said his Irish Litany. In thirty-two years he never once missed it. It was almost as long as all the other prayers put together, and growing longer every year. Luckily for him Dr. Healy had not taken to writing till his day was over.[2] Had he, it would have been another 'case,' and would have given the wise and good Superior at least several racking headaches, before he would have succeeded in solving it in his own noble fashion.

When he was near his end, poor fellow, the community gathered round his bed and recited the usual prayers for the dying. When they came to the Litany of the Saints, " Stop ! " he cried, and began himself:

" St. Patrick, Apostle and Patron of Ireland,"

" St. Brigid, Patroness of Ireland,"

" St. Columbkille," and went on and on strongly to the end; the community, most of them in tears, sobbing the responses as best they could. " Now," said he weakly, " you can bring in the foreigners." They began again. But before they were half through, Brother 'Tony was with his own beloved Irish saints in heaven.

May he rest in peace ! [3]

---

[1] This poor Leitrim fellow, Tom McGowan, is blind from birth, and cared for in this charitable institution for the past forty years. Everything that came within the range of his knowledge for the last fifty years is as fresh in his memory as if it happened but yesterday, even to the day of the week and the kind of the day. Ask him, for instance, what day of the week did the 6th of May, 1861, fall on ? What sort of a day was it ? You get without a pause both answers absolutely correctly. When did Cardinal McCabe die ? When did Queen Victoria visit Dublin ? When was I here last ? What did I talk about ? On the spot you get day and date and all the details you want. Once he hears a date or fact, or it comes under his observation, he simply cannot forget it. And the writer was introduced to him, not by a Brother Azevedo, but by a Brother Patrick !

[2] And, of course, he had never come across such works as Colgan's, or the MSS. of O'Clery or of Aengus, which still remain as MSS.

[3] His history is quite true in substance. This is the utmost we can say at present. But nobody in his senses ever guaranteed verbal accuracy in quoting Dame Gamplet. She is still, we understand, down in the west, as alive and aliveike as was ever the famous Mrs. Harris.

Chapter IX

TOWNS CRADLED IN HERMITS' CELLS

ORIGIN OF THE NAME CASTLEDERMOT—ORIGIN OF DYSERT-DIARMADA, NAME AND PLACE—SIMILAR ORIGIN OF KILDARE, NAME AND PLACE—OF ROSCOMMON—ROSCREA—MONASTEREVIN AND ABBEYLEIX—ATHY—CLOYNE—CORK—FORT AUGUSTUS IN OUR OWN DAYS.

THOUGH elsewhere holding its own fairly well, in Leinster *dysert* had often to give way to *castle*—we hope only temporarily. No doubt in Anglo-Norman days such strongholds bulked large in the eyes of the poor natives. The names were often in their mouths, and, poor things, the terror—not the love—of them often in their hearts. There is no reason, we can see, why it should be so any longer.

Strongbow, having to do with other people's property, "bestowed" with a liberal hand possessions on his followers. To Walter de Riddlesford he gave the lands of Murthy and Imayle in which Dysert-Diarmada stood. This was the ancient patrimony of the O'Tooles or O'Tohills. Their chief used to be inaugurated at the Chair of Kildare town. St. Laurence O'Toole was of the clan. His mother, it may be added, was an O'Byrne, so he is out and out *Kildarensis*. Moreover, he was born (in 1123) quite close to Dysert-Diarmada, within sound of its Round Tower bell. The castle connoted in Castledermot, the new appellation, was built either by this de Riddlesford, or by his son-in-law and heir, the third Lord Offaly. Authorities are not at one on the matter. Hence the name is comparatively modern.

The ancient and more correct name of the town, Dysert-Diarmada, goes back at least some four or five hundred years further. It is due to the circumstance that about 800 A.D. according to Joyce, or about 500 A.D. according to Comer-

ford, Archdall, and others, Diarmad,[1] son of Aedh Roin, King of Ulidia (Ulster), selected the spot, then a lonely waste, for his cell. Around the cell a monastery, with school attached, grew; and then around the monastery a town.
This origin and development of our old towns is not uncommon. It is well worth delaying to notice it.

KILDARE itself, for instance, grew around St. Brigid's home beneath the spreading oak tree. (Kill-dara=the church of the oak.)

Here, about the year 487, she made her cell in her father's territory. Animosus, Bishop of Kildare, writing towards the close of the tenth century, that is five hundred years afterwards, tells us that the trunk of this "goodly faire oke" still remains, "for Brigid loved it much and blessed it, and no one dares cut it with a weapon." St. Brigid's cell increased into her celebrated conventual establishment. A little later it expanded into a large town. "Long before her death, which occurred about the year 525," writes Hyde, "a great city and a school rivalling the fame of Armagh itself, had risen round her oak-tree." Figuratively speaking—and the metaphor forces itself on one—Brigid's cell was the planted acorn, Kildare town the full-grown oak. Subsequently the whole county took its title from the town, and honoured itself by thus associating itself with the memory of the "Mary of the Gael." No county in Ireland is more happily named.

ROSCOMMON, indeed, we should say in fairness as we have been contrasting them, rivals it. It means Comon's wood (*ros*), and is called after St. Comon. Comon founded a monastery where the town of Roscommon now stands, either in the middle of the sixth or in the beginning of the eighth century.[2] A town, of course, sprung up about the monastery, and later on the county adopted the town's designation. Here again we have the four steps in the ladder of progress, a hermit's hut, a monastery, a town, a county.

In the North Riding of Tipperary there is a town akin

---

[1] Otherwise called Ainle because of his fresh complexion.—Healy.
[2] The Four Masters record his death under the year 746 or 747, but other authorities place him much earlier.

in sound and significance, ROSCREA. Roscrea can be traced back to its origin in an anchorite's little cell almost as clearly as can the Boyne water to storied Trinity Well at the foot of Carbury Hill. This Kildare fountain, the Helicon Spring of Keltic sagas and mythology, is by the way now looked after as such celebrated wells should be, by Mr. Robinson of Newberry Hall, on whose property it stands. All honour be to such as he.

The Rev. Baring-Gould in his Protestant " Lives of the [Catholic] Saints," gives in a nut-shell the history of Roscrea :

> About the year 615, [he states], St. Cronan erected a cell near the lake or marsh of Crea, which was called Seaurius [Seanross beside Corville House]. The cause of his leaving it was this. Some strangers who came to pay him a visit, were not able to find it out, and in their wanderings remained a whole night on the bog without food or roof to shelter them. This so distressed Cronan that he determined to quit his lonesome spot [*desertus et avius* it is elsewhere described], and he removed to the high road [from Meath to Munster], where he erected a large monastery, which in the course of time gave rise to the town of Roscrea.[1]

Doubtless it fared with St. Cronan's new home as it did with most other religious houses in Ireland.

> When a monastery prospered, [states the late Dr. O'Rorke of Achonry in his "History of Sligo" and the Sligo gentry], population flowed towards it : consisting, first, of young persons who came to join the community as novices ; secondly, of such lay persons as were wanted for agricultural or other works, always in progress about the place ; thirdly, of the poor and sick, who were fed, and clothed, and cared, by the religious ;[2] and fourthly, as in the case of Armagh, Bangor, Clonfert, Lismore, and other large establishments, famed for their schools, by students whom love of learning attracted from other parts of the country, and even from other countries.[3]

Dr. O'Rorke is here speaking of Drumcliff. This was a Sligo monastic establishment which, as he shows, for centuries

---

[1] Vol. IV. April 28th, p. 361. Dr. Healy's account is substantially the same, but fuller—" Ancient Schools," p. 523. Count O'Byrne of Corville, it should be recorded to his credit, as carefully preserves Cronan's old *damliagh* from injury or profanation as does Mr. Robinson, Trinity Well.

[2] That is, they were Infirmaries, Hospitals, Hospices, and Dispensaries, no less than Charitable Institutions and undegrading Homes for the afflicted young and the homeless aged.

[3] Vol. I., p. 497.

did its work so quietly and silently—as all great men and great institutions do—that it was only by accident that the rest of Ireland learned of its existence. The new Cistercian Abbey and College of Mount St. Joseph, Roscrea, within a mile or two of St. Cronan's ancient little dwelling, are trying to do equally good work for God and country, and in the unostentatious spirit, too, of Drumcliff of Columbkille. There is no advertising. History repeats itself.

MONASTEREVIN in Kildare and ABBEYLEIX in Queen's County need no commentary. St. Evin was a contemporary of St. Patrick. There was nothing of a town here on the banks of the Barrow in his day. According to Colgan it was he who wrote the *Tripartite Life of St. Patrick*. But this opinion has not withstood the research and criticism of recent years.

The second mentioned name, it should be said, is noteworthy. The title of the O'More territory was Laeghis. This is pronounced Leesh, but was known in later degenerate days as Leix. It figures very conspicuously in Irish and Anglo-Irish chronicles. It is now extinct; first debased and then immolated by ignorance and anglicisation. But it is still preserved, as a martyr's bones in a silver shrine, we may venture to say, in the one compound, Abbeyleix. The Abbey was founded in 1183, and owed its existence to the piety and munificence of the O'More of the day.

Unlike Monasterevin, the designation of still another town in Kildare, and it the largest, prompts no suspicion that it, too, had an ecclesiastical origin. All the same it had.

ATHY (older Ath-I), one of our few passably anglicised place-names, as rare as white blackbirds, means the ford (ath) [1] of Ae (Aedh). The ford was a noted one, leading from the principality of the O'Mores or O'Moores, just referred to, to Hy-Murray of Kildare, the territory of the O'Tooles. Aedh (the final letters are idle in the pronunciation) was a famous Munster chief. He was slain at the

---

[1] Ath in France was the last town taken by a Highland regiment just before the signing of the Armistice. The name, typical of thousands of others on the Continent, tells its own story of the far-flung Kelt, and of the early colonisation of Gaul by the Kelts.

beginning of the second century in a rere-guard action. For, unlike the leader of a modern army, an Irish chieftain—here we have one example of it and history supplies hundreds —when his kerns and galloglasses were overwhelmed and routed, never entrusted the post where the fight, into which he had led them, was fiercest to a subordinate; and he scorned at the expense of others to try and save his own skin. Their bravery burnished brightest in danger and in disaster. A rhyme is current in Ulster that

> The O'Doherties tall
> From dark Donegal
> Were the last from the field that retreated.

The special glory of the clan O'Doherty was a glory also claimed by every Irish King and Tanist, from Aedh to the last of them. Athy, which he resolutely defended to save his fleeing followers from slaughter and where he fell, was the pass over the Barrow.

It was nothing more. And such it remained for eleven hundred years afterwards. As a town—we quote again from a Protestant writer—"it owes its foundation to two monasteries erected on each side of the river at the entrance of an extensive wood, in the thirteenth century. . . . Hence," he states, "from these two monasteries the place was denominated. . . . Bla Theagh, pronounced Blahai, or the town of the two houses, which name it still retains in Irish.[1]"

The founders of one monastery, the Dominican, were the Boisels and Hogans, and of the other, the Crouched friars', Richard de St. Michael, Lord of Rheban. May it be added, however, that when abbeys and churches were erected out of their Irish plunder by Norman adventurers, an Irishman's laudation can hardly be expected to be pitched in a high key. A farmer's exclamation about his sanctimonious and not over-scrupulous neighbour may best express our appreciation of Richard de St. Michael, Lord of Rheban's generosity : " May the Lord bless him ! Why, he'd stale a cow, and give the horns away for the love of God." In these pages very little is said about objects of such Norman munificence. Silence is sometimes golden.

The town was English. Towards the close of the fifteenth

---

[1] " B " in *The Anthologia Hibernica*, May, 1793, p. 325, etc. We are justified in assuming that all its contributors were of the religion of ascendancy .

6

century, as it commanded this important ford, it became a frontier garrison town of the contracted Pale. The monks were English, Catholic, of course. The residents were English, and they were petted and patted beyond measure. In and around the town, castles and jails and whipping-posts and sundry other marks and tokens of civilisation sprung up as rapidly as scarecrows in a planted field, or as drinking-booths in a cattle-green on a fair-day morning. Assizes were held. Nay, by an Act of Henry VII, they could be held nowhere else in the county except here or in Naas. To make assurance doubly sure the Act was solemnly and solidly buttressed by a supplementary proviso, perfectly Irish in its style perhaps you will say, viz., that it should remain in force then and forever—until repealed. Is it that the wise Solons of this Tudor monarch had been, despite themselves, unconsciously imbibing of the Irish spirit and oversaid it ? Or is it that, distinctly prophetic no less than wise, they saw the shadow of coming, though then far distant, events, and of Athy, as it is now, thoroughly Irish, and were in advance legislating for it, and preparing to withdraw their sunny smiles ? Nobody can decide. A Solon as wise as one of themselves alone could declare which theory is right.

But anyway Assizes were regularly held in Athy. Men were put in the stocks. Every six months culprits by the score were hanged at the very least ; for these were the days when Irishmen got used to the process. Even the monks of the place were not without the luxury of petty law-suits between themselves now and again as well as another. Rheban (anciently Raiba, it means the Royal Abode) on the west bank of the Barrow, was in the second century one of Ireland's inland cities. It had a celebrated fair, held yearly on St. Michael's Day. The fair was quashed, or rather the venue changed to this favoured Assize town, as the relics of Carman to Naas. Various tolls and customs and pickings *à l'anglaise* were introduced and upheld.

Further, in 1615, on Athy was bestowed the gift of a charter consituting it a borough. It sent its two members to Parliament, and was governed at home " by a recorder, sovereign, two bailiffs, and a town clerk." Under such an array of magnates and Areiopagites, including the town clerk, we may be sure that law and order was scrupulously observed. It had its 'Sovereign's Court' to enforce it. It enjoyed, besides, all the privileges and immunities, commercial, social, and even religious, that could be showered upon it. No step-mother's breath was over it. It prospered.

Athy, you see, is Anglo-Norman, and its progress sheds no halo on Irish endeavour. Of the two thirteenth century friaries, which were its initial buildings, scarcely a trace remained as far back as 1793, except a postern gate of one of them, stupidly called Preston's Gate. Besides, it is not an old town, as the adjective is understood in this ancient country. Hence, apart from its origin being radically religious, in a sense, and Catholic, an Irishman's interest in it is not of the keenest. For further information, should the reader be athirst for it, in Rawson's " Statistical Survey of Kildare," or perhaps in Comerford, we would respectfully recommend him go look for it.

CLOYNE, in Cork, is a small little place as compared to Athy. It is but a village, though a pretty one. Yet had it been favoured at any time with a charter like Athy's it could with absolute correctness be described as a city. For it was for long and long the place of a Bishop's See ; and that is a city's main feature, indeed the sole feature legally distinguishing it from a common borough town.

The name of the village or, as we should like to say, of the little cathedral city, comes down to us from pre-historic times. As usual in Keltic nomenclature it is apt. It is no empty title. Cloyne=Cluan-Namha, and Cluan-Namha may be translated, the Plain of the Caves. These caves with their subterranean river are still to be seen in the old Bishop's palace grounds. About 2,000 years ago, perhaps about the time that Herod the Great was reigning in Palestine, though it may have been long before, the intelligent old pagan Cork men were struck by them, and connoted them in the name they gave the plain.

" A hermitage, growing into a monastery and eventually into a bishop's seat, originated this little town." So testifies the President of the Royal Society of Antiquaries, Mr. Westropp.[1] Accordingly, though Cloyne is small, in both

---

[1] *Journal, R.S.A.I.*, Vol. VII. 5th Series, p. 337. To it we are indebted for many of the facts about Cloyne.

its origin and its title its honour is great. St. Colman Mac Lenin (*c.* 522-601), a descendant of the famous King, Leth Mhoge, who was the rival and of course the contemporary of Conn of the Hundred Battles, and who gave his name to the southern half of Erin, was the hermit and founder. As there are a score and more of St. Colmans he has to get his family title, Mac Lenin. He was a man of saintly life of course; but besides that he was a poet and an historian. So famed was he on all three counts that three centuries after his death the King-Bishop Cormac Mac Culenain, reputed to be, to use an old annalist's words, " the most learned of all who came or shall come of the men of Erin for ever," desired in his will to be buried in Cloyne beside him. Like St. Ignatius Loyola and St. Thomas Aquinas he sprung from a martial race, too. A quaint passage in " The Wars of the Gael and Gall "[1] would throw some doubt on their valour; for it alleges that three hundred and forty-three of them were only " equal to one Hector of Troy who equalled sixteen thousand eight hundred and seven Murchad O'Briens." But most likely this is only low and interested disparagement of both the Mac Lenins and the O'Briens.

St. Colman's Cathedral, a cruciform Catholic structure mainly of the thirteenth century, still adorns Cloyne. It has been modernised, the plastering and whitewashing hiding away, it is said, richly ornamented capitals; and " restored," too, and well spoiled likewise in the doing of it, like almost all our ' appropriated ' churches. Of course, at the very outstart they were no more suited for the new worship than a town hall for a jail. Much damage had to be done. But despite it all, their original purpose breaks through. The philosopher Berkeley officiated here from 1734 to 1752. He was an Irishman, born at Dysert Castle on the Nore. One wonders, though, was he really an Irishman seeing that he became a bishop, and in the days when all Protestant bishops were imported, and when political " pull " rather than merit or ability determined the selection.

A Round Tower stands not far from the Cathedral. You can almost touch it as you pass down the little street. Most probably it is just beside the exact site of a previous St. Colman's church, for quite close to a church or an ecclesi-

---

[1] p. 187.

astical establishment is their invariable position. Round Towers were erected certainly not by the Danes but principally against them; as places of refuge in their sudden raids, and consequently mainly during the period when the country was exposed to these incursions (eighth to eleventh century).[1] In any case, they were put up centuries and centuries before Luther was born, or the religion made-in-Germany was adopted by the English schismatics.

Confiscated churches and overshadowing Round Towers make, then, ill-matched pairs. The latter are silent witnesses telling of a previous wholly Catholic period. And they are sad witnesses, too, for they seem to say: " We, indeed, protected monk and priest and sacred vessels and holy relic and everything they valued against the Danish Hun; but alas! we were helpless against the later more subtle spoliator."

The Catholic cathedral is now, we may say, rebuilt in Queenstown. Its interior leaves the impression that there are millionaires about, so gorgeous is it. But exteriorly it is a stately modern edifice, whose graceful white limestone spire, sparkling in the sunshine, is the first object to greet the home-returning exile. For all that, the old and lowly village-city of St. Colman is to us much more interesting than the showy city seated on the hill, yclept since the famine years by the name royal. Why such fine old names as The Cove and Dunleary, with all their poetic and historic associations, should be scrapped and discarded, stands sorely in need of an adequate explanation. How their town can be called Kingstown or Queenstown by good Irish Irishmen, and how their church can be called St. Mary's or St. Colman's by pious Protestants, who obey their first and sixth commandments as they understand them, are twin puzzles it were wiser not try to probe into too deeply. Bishop Berkeley himself, were he alive, could scarcely

---

[1] Petrie gives several good reasons for believing that some of them are as early as at least the sixth or seventh century. Originally they were intended according to him, as church belfries—bells have been in modern days hung up in several of them, including this one at Cloyne—and perhaps also as church castles, for protection when danger threatened. At all events in Danish days this second purpose predominated. It was this that insured a good height above the ground for the entrance. As a belfry it would be a drawback.

If the comparison be not too profane, a blackthorn is for one manifest use. But occasionally it is put to another. At times numbers of them are cut and prepared with special care for that other alone.

solve them without raking up facts from the embers of the past whose smouldering existence both find it convenient, perhaps, to ignore. Let sleeping snakes sleep on. Young Terence Casey, the hero of Glenanaar, used to spout Davis' most patriotic poems and his soul was attune to them. It were better far for him, poor fellow, had he never learned to see any incongruity in it.

The city of CORK itself was also cradled in a hermit's cell. St. Finbarr or Barry, who died about 630, and of whom, according to Ware, St. Colman was a disciple, was the hermit. After spending some years in a wild solitude, on an islet in a lake near the source of the Lee (which lake has ever since been called after him Gougane Barra, *i.e.*, Barry's Lone Retreat), he fled away from its superb but distracting beauties. Following on down the pleasant waters of the same river he came at last to a great swampy 'dysert' near its mouth, as lonely and almost as inaccessible as sea-girt Iona or Lindisfarne or Inishmurray.

This marsh was so extensive that it was entitled then, and for many hundred years afterwards, Corcach-mor-Mumhan, *i.e.*, the Great-Marsh-of-Munster. It was still there as late as 1600 as is evident from old maps. The long compound, Corcach-mor-Mumhan, shrivelled and shrivelled, as is the way with much used words, until nothing now remains but its first syllable, Corc. This serves and suffices to designate the sturdy rebel city on the Lee, and we may be fairly confident it will become no shorter.

But its nucleus was a religious house. In the first years of the seventh century on the edge of this lonely swamp, St. Finbarr, fleeing away from Gougane Barra, discovered a cave to shelter him. Of this he made his humble dwelling. Undistracted by scenic beauties, undisturbed save by the whirr of the wild duck or by the evening bleat of the *minnaun airigh*, he settled down in it to live his life of prayer and penance and close union with God. But it wasn't to be as he had planned it. Man proposes but God disposes. The history of the very word, monastery—it primarily means the dwelling-place of a solitary, living in seclusion—suggests what happened. Soon he had to build a Religious House, and to it " as to the home of wisdom and the nursery of all Christian virtues, crowds of zealous disciples flocked from all quarters."[1] To supply their wants a town grew about the monastery. Subsequently the town expanded into a city, the city of the Shandon bells. Thus did Cork from a solitude become a city. Later this city, as in the cases just mentioned, gave its name to the wide-extending county.

The four steps again ; cell—monastery—city—county.

Even our own days have witnessed similar, if more rapid, developments.

Some forty years ago FORT AUGUSTUS was an inaccessible spot in the heart of the Highlands of Scotland ; railwayless, almost roadless, as tenantless as lonely Rannockmoor which is not quite so far north. You might be there deer-stalking for days and days and, as we phrase it in Ireland, never meet a sinner. Then, in 1880 to be exact, the monks went thither, just as St. Finbarr, twelve or thirteen centuries before, made his way to the Great Marsh of Munster.

There is an Order in the Church which was founded " in the gloom of the long past," a hundred years before St. Finbarr's eyes rested on lone Gougane Barra, or his feet trod deep-valleyed Desmond. It is still in the strength and vigour of its early prime. It cherishes to-day its sainted founder, Benedict's, love of prayer and of solitude. Men from the noisy tramway- and trolley-ridden cities, who go to visit its hospitable, secluded English Houses, often stay awake of nights listening to the silence. The Benedictines went to Fort Augustus. They founded a monastery by the wild-deer tracks on the southern shore of Lough Ness. It was far from the hum and taint of the world, as far as anywhere still in the British Isles could nowadays possibly be.

But the world followed them. Already Fort Augustus is a flourishing little town. A steamer from Inverness comes and goes every day by the twenty-mile-long lake. A Highland railway has climbed up, up, fifty miles and more up, its track sheltered in places from the deluging winter snows by corrugated-iron roofing, up from lonely Craigenlaragh ; just that far and no further. The tower and minarets of a stately church are now seen above the tree tops on Loch

---

[1] " Ireland's Ancient Schools and Scholars," by Dr. Healy, p. 480.

Ness's margin. Morning, noon, and night, the angelus bell is heard,

> "O'er the wide watered shore,
> Swinging slow with solemn roar,"

the sound of its tolling dying away on the rippling waters, and amid the shaggy woods and craggy heathery mountains. Not three times a day, but practically all day long, to the accompaniment of a pealing organ, the magnificent liturgical services of the Church are rendered in the superb fashion for which the Benedictines, the parent Order of all Orders, are without a rival in the Church.

In other words a monastery was planted in a 'dysert,' a town grows around the monastery; and the history of the long-ago in Ireland, the history of Kildare and Roscommon, of Roscrea, Monasterevin and Abbeyleix, of Cork and of Castledermot, of Kilkenny [1] and of half a hundred others, repeats itself before our very eyes in the sister, Keltic still Catholic Scotland.

---

[1] The parent of *Cill* or *Kill*, as of all Irish ecclesiastical terms, is the Latin. This constancy in origin tells clearly its own tale of whence came our Christianity. *Cill* is derived from, or, we might almost say, is the self-same as the Latin *cella*, and *cella* has the signification, church. Next to *baile*, *cill* is the most prolific root of Irish place-names. There are as many as 2,700 of them, according to Joyce, whose first syllable is *Cill*, either quite apparent or more or less disguised. In the greater number, as in the above instance in the text,—Kilkenny=the church of St. Canice—the founder or patron's name is blended in the compound.

These few facts are quite as good as half-a-dozen logically written chapters in vindication of the title, The Island of Saints.

Chapter X

A DUEL BETWEEN NAMES

DYSERT-DIARMADA OR CASTLEDERMOT, WHICH WINS ?—THE FIRST SCORES ON SOUND AND ON DERIVATION.

"Words are *things*, as well as the symbols of things."
—" English Grammar," by Rev. Canon Daniel, Preface, p. 1.

FROM what has been written up to this the necessary inference, we submit, is that the ancient name Dysert-Diarmada is better than the modern one Castledermot.

Castle should go down tumbling before Dysert. Dysert alone and of itself should insure it a triumph. In view of all we have seen that this word imports, all the religious and national associations that crowd and cluster round it and all the brightening and comforting memories it recalls, it is scarcely too extravagant to transfer to it one of the silver-tongued Moore's most beautiful similes, and say of it, that in the hearing of a Catholic Irishman it is,

"As whispered balm, as sunshine spoken."

But let us compare them further.

Regarding them on their merits as mere words, or things in Canon Daniel's sense, Dysert-Diarmada is our choice. It is more grateful to the ear : it is as beautifully alliterative as Dysert O'Dea ; it is as full-vowelled as Creevelea or Gougane Barra, as Minnesota or Tennessee or any of the old un-Anglican American place-names. It sounds, we may say, as if writ on satin and goes trippingly on the tongue. Castledermot, on the other hand, is a comparatively offensive combination of consonants hissing and cawing at you. More than that, the first of the two component parts does not so well liquefy into the second. There is a perceptible incompatability between them ; a jolt as you pass from one to the other ; a hitch or gasp between the two constituents, and the whole, one would fancy, could be best said by a man with a chronic cough. Writing them as one word does not mend matters. The hiatus is there and cannot be hidden.

An acquaintance of ours is surnamed Muggins. He so hates and detests the name that when away from about home he always calls himself Malone. The case before us is not quite as bad as that, we admit, but the exaggeration will bring out the idea. A harsh-sounding name grates like a loud, ill-mannered voice. It is as offensive to the trained ear as is roughness or uncouthness of address to the well brought up. " A man may be a man for a' that," you declare. True enough. But then that means, despite all that. Why put on a heavy handicap ? We frame the photograph of a valued friend not in white deal but in polished mahogany or something equally sightly; an amethyst is usually set in gold, never in lead or copper. A beautiful name does not make a town beautiful, but it conveys the first and most lasting impression. A beautiful name becomes a beautiful town. If at hand why not use it ? Edinburgh would be something less than Edinburgh if called Glāsko. Your pretty suburban villa residence, Fern Lodge, would never be deemed so select and charming, at least unless by your visitors, if the address on your stationery read, No. 16, Blank Street. Dysert-Diarmada, as a town, suits, we hope, its beautiful name. Friend Malone is right on principle.

Castledermot, however, considered as a Dictionary word or pure object, has not even the merit of being strikingly repulsive and ill-sounding. Its second and better half saves it from that. Were it—like for instance, Ploopluck, near Naas, or Jigginstown,[1] also beside it, or like Muggins itself— it would be more tolerable. For there are tastes that can admire anything roundly *outré*. The beauty of a wrinkle-faced, bandy-legged bull-dog, for instance, is his ugliness ; the beauty of a German dachshund or turnspit, his grotesqueness and absurdity. But who could endure the combination of a battered silk hat and a new and neat Chesterfield coat ? of a squatty tower and a graceful Gothic church ? Like Castledermot the ill-assorted whole would be odious to every taste, good, bad, and indifferent.

---

[1] Here are the ruins of a mansion, which was begun by the unfortunate Earl of Strafford. There is also a Gigginstown in Westmeath, which is a lough ; and a Jenkinstown in Meath, which too is not a town but a house.

Again on their merits as mere words, on derivation or descent Dysert-Diarmada wins.

This ancient term, as we have already shown, is to be regarded as pure Irish. But the modern one, Castledermot, grammarians would unhesitatingly brand as a hybrid. Literally that means that it is a word of shame—a mule word. It is neither fish nor flesh, neither Irish nor English, but half one, half the other.

The stigma branded upon it may be better appreciated by a little consideration.

A fancier, it is said, cannot tolerate a dog about his place, be he ever so wise or playful or in appearance majestic, unless he is full-bred something. He may be any species you like, from a St. Bernard to a toy Pom.; but he must be that. He has no use for a mongrel—except to make a present of him. Those who take a genuine interest in horses, poultry, anything—canaries if you like—have or develop more or less the same instinct.

You reading this, in your carpet slippers with a Dictionary at your elbow, may be quite unconscious of this intuition. You may pride and plume yourself on being above all such rude and unintellectual vanities. You may have looked up superciliously from the page where you saw the word " dog," and failed to find the phrase " the friend of man " tripping after it by way of apology for its use. You might, should a dog appear on your horizon, hurl your carpet slipper after him if you hadn't the tongs. Well, for our part, we are not a bit inclined to say, so much the better for you. Everybody, thank goodness, is not so. Remember that such tastes make the world a little brighter for very many. They afford pleasure and, what is less likely to be misappreciated, profit—occasionally—to thousands upon thousands, quite a number of whom might also claim to be Solomons; quite a number of whom are, too, whether by good luck or good guiding, successful men as the world goes, and therefore can forthwith put on their ready-made characters of Solomons. Life is a diamond with many facettes. No two men see things through precisely the same pair of glasses. So in the world there is less elbowing aside and less jostling. It is large enough for the whole of us. Dr. Syntax's day-dream may be to write a glorious Epic. Tom Towser may be equally keen on possessing a champion Irish terrier. From their different points of view each is equally reasonable. Between both ambitions there is little to choose. Both are perhaps equally laudable. Not even when one is in a mood cynical, or has a bad toothache, should he dare allow such an opinion pass his lips as that they are equally absurd or nonsensical. By all means let the children have the toys that amuse them. Let them gather the shells by the sea-shore an it please them. Let them play in the sunshine God has given them. He would be a fool for his pains that would cast a shadow over it. A hundred years from now, there will be for them neither toys, nor shells, nor sunshine.

But Carpet Slippers must also be aware from his reading that even little dogs were not always despised and " shooed." Greece in the days of Plato was as highly intellectual a spot of earth as culture has yet produced. It was the University of the civilised world. It contained many philosophers, a few of whom, it will be readily conceded, were half as wise as any of us. Is it not upon one of them that the paradox is fathered : it is unwise to be too wise ? Not a philosopher of them ever took a peripatetic walk without a dog at his heels. In that enlightened age if a man went abroad in the streets of Athens so unaccompanied, he would be stared at quite as much (we don't say as unmercifully, for Dubliners, like Athenians, are too polite for that) as if Carpet Slippers put on him, came out and marched down O'Connell Street in his freshly-brushed silk hat off the hall-stand, but minus his dress coat—in his shirt sleeves. It is safe enough to say that the best sentences Demosthenes ever uttered were spoken to his little Gyp, or Rebel or Argos or White Fang, or whatever he called him.

Whether dignified or not, however, the illustration if, as rhetoricians exact, it does not serve to ennoble the theme, at all events it does illustrate, and that is the main thing.

Grammarians and philologists—*i.e.*, experts in language or word-fanciers (Carpet Slippers we feel sure is among them)—are a far more numerous class than dog-fanciers— not comparing them. (This old grandmother's phrase might after all have best saved the situation, had we thought of it in time.) Those who take an intelligent interest in the language they speak are a further allied body almost as numberless as the politicians. For it includes not merely

A DUEL BETWEEN NAMES 93

University Professors, School Ma'ams and School Monitors, but all speakers and writers, as well as all who put up to be in any sense educated—as education is conventionally understood in this country.[1] Combining the two allied classes into one they constitute a number, as Shakespeare would say, " beyond arithmetic."

Now, the minds of the whole lot are haunted by the same obsessions anent barbarisms and solecisms. Every one of them has precisely the same *animus* against hybrid words that the canine fancier entertains for what he opprobiously calls cur-dogs—" not comparing them." The greater the expert the more pronounced the feeling. A pure French or a pure Brazilian term, for instance, if wanted, he will take, after some demur, into his vocabulary. Reluctantly we must say. But a heterogeneously descended compound, never. There are, indeed, too many of them already in the language. But that cannot now be helped. Old dogs are mercifully let be, live or die.

The English tongue itself is in another sense a mongrel among the languages. But people have to make the best of it now. Like England itself it, let us say, ' appropriated ' from every nation. Being now very wealthy, in the sense of having amassed in its Dictionaries some hundreds of thousands of pounds—we mean words—the English are complacently satisfied about it, and vote it the best of all possible tongues. Nobody but themselves thinks so. A language always—it is a well-worn saying—portrays the character and reflects the history of the people who speak and use it. Like a well-tailored coat, it best suits those whose it is, however badly it becomes others.

Now offer a sportsman a young Gordon Setter. He will be delighted. Send him a present of a Setter-Collie. Your errand-boy will have back your present, declined, with of course a good excuse and profuse thanks. " So sorry— extremely grateful—fearfully overcrowded kennels," or something like that.

Similarly, show the two words whose merits we are com-

---

[1] *Viz.*, knowing the *English* language, it does not matter a brass button what else you don't know. Should you have the distinction of speaking it with a Cockney accent, all you want besides is to be of some non-Catholic brand of religion, and you are ready and all for a Sub-Inspectorship of the R.I.C. or a Resident Magistracy.

paring to any genuine Skeats or Peile or Weekley or Max Müller, to any literary Professor or Word-Fancier, and request him tell you which should you keep for your vocabulary, which is the better. You need have no hesitation in troubling one of them. Good scholars are always gentlemanly; easily talked to, ever ready to oblige, most truthful, as well as necessarily humble. It is only the conscious frauds that put on aloofness and pomposity and a haw-haw accent as a kind of defensive armour. And it is often very much needed. For that matter have the opinion of any man worth his salt of the vast combined class above indicated as to which is the better word. " Certainly Dysert-Diarmada," will be his prompt answer. " What then, please, should I do with this nice word Castledermot ? " " Do away with it," will be his equally decided response.

In the correlative case we once heard a sensible countryman give the self-same answer, though in his own homely phrases. " What are you to do with that beauty, is it ? Mushah, what do you want with it ? Haven't you another and a better ? Tie a stone round its neck and take it to the nearest bog-hole."

Chapter XI
DYSERT-DIARMADA WINS AS A PLACE-NAME

TAKING them up as mere Dictionary words, we have seen that Dysert-Diarmada scores both in euphony and on derivation. As a mere word still, there is a third and more serious particular in which it beats Castledermot hollow, *viz.*, as a place-designation. This is important because it touches on their very essence and marrow.

A fiery Frenchman, Henri Estienne, once reproved his countrymen for letting in Italian terms. "Adopt," he advised them, "only Italian words which express Italian qualities hitherto unknown to the French, such as *charlatan, assassin, poltron.*" That this was centuries before the *Entente* was heard of, is an easy inference. The advice was good and, quite unconsciously to the passionately patriotic Frenchman, witty.

Common nouns such as those given are, however, from one point of view very fleeting things, as evanescent as perfumes or puffs of smoke. They are said and they are gone. "A breath can make them as a breath has made." If there be anything of permanency at all in words it is in proper nouns, more especially in place-names. Mountains' titles, for instance, are almost as old as the mountains themselves; as old we mean as the first man that saw them, and was struck by their grandeur, and bowed down before the majesty of the great Creator who made them. Mountains, like the semi-mythical heroes or demi-gods, emerge from the misty past and the dark hinterlands of history fully named. The significance of these designations can only be explained, if at all, from the speech of the primitive inhabitants. Men may come and men may go but the mountains and their names, more imperishable than the mythical chiefs or than any tongue or tribe or people, remain forever. These are facts and there is no use delaying to philosophise about them. The principle as a principle holds good for all place-designations, with exceptions of course to prove the rule. A merciless, exterminating conquest alone has a chance, and it's only a chance, of wiping them out. The Shannon was the Shannon in the time of Ptolemy. The Shannon would be the Shannon still, had Cromwell elected to drive all the Irishry, including those of his selected province, into the first of the two places indicated in his famous alternative, and had his drive been, in his eyes, a complete success.

If it is bad then for a nation to change its language, to change its place-names is ten times worse. It shows a refinement in subserviency of which not even really and thoroughly conquered peoples, not excepting the Indians of North America or the Maoris, have ever been guilty. To christening cities that are founded by the enterprise, or have risen to eminence by the fostering care of invaders who made a new land their home and threw in their lot with its inhabitants, there can be no reasonable objection. They have a right to name their own offspring. But alas! where are such in Ireland? "The symbols of attempted conquest are roofless castles, ruined abbeys and confiscated cathedrals,"[1] and, we may add, not new but decaying ancient towns.

It further follows that it is even unfair to "The Last Conquest of Ireland, Perhaps," to get rid of the old place-names. For it would argue a ruthless and wholesale annihilation. This did not happen. Let us be perfectly just, they were not as bad as that. Sometimes it could not come off. Sometimes, too, the still proud natives, whose resistance was in one way and another battered down, were found useful, nay indispensable, as diggers and delvers; later on as rent-payers; later still, for it was in them all the time, as fearless fighters. Manifestly to assert or insinuate that they were mercilessly and to a man exterminated, would be nothing short of gross detraction.

Recurring now to our definite example, Dysert-Diarmada stands where it stood 600, aye, 800, 1,000, years ago. It is no better but much worse as to importance and numbers. It was then called Dysert-Diarmada. Those who now call

---

[1] Mansion House Address against Conscription.

it Castledermot—or, we greatly fear, simply the Castle—are speaking unmanfully and very, very, subserviently. Besides they are not speaking fairly or generously. Must we put it clearer, " not judging them," and declare that they are uttering what contains implicitly a calumnious falsehood ?

You may retort, they have in what they term it the old as well as the new. We reply, perhaps so. Personally we do not know. We have only our own deep reasons for suspecting. But granted that they never drop the reminiscence of Diarmad contained in the corrupted form -dermot, and never by any chance say bluntly, the Castle. Anything is better than nothing, and we are thankful for small mercies. But even so, the combination of the new and the old is an incongruity and an absurdity. It reminds one of a clown's coat, partly grey or green and partly a heathery purple.

You may urge again : They made a compromise as sensible people always do. They will have it half and half, English and Irish. We reply : Save us from our friends! For once they recognise that they will repudiate it. History, present and past, justifies the utmost confidence in the men of Kildare. They are not milk-and-water. To return to our old illustration they have no respect, nor love nor liking, for a dog that trots a bit of the road with everybody. Bogholes are plentiful. The Shannon, we believe, will be the Shannon till the crack of doom. But work on your half-way-house principle and it may yet become Mumbo-Jumbo.

Henri Estienne's advice, then, is sound. It is wise as well as witty. The kernel of it is, to hold fast to your own and to eschew new-fangled names, unless, of course, they be needed for new things.

There is a want, indeed, in Irish, too, we have it on the best authority, for good terms for *charlatan, poltroon, diplomat, shoneen*. But there is no dearth of words expressive of bravery, honesty, suffering, self-sacrifice, devotion—nor is there any need whatever, good or bad, for fresh place-names. A language, it is quite true, demonstrates the character of the people who speak and use it. But let us not sail off in the clouds, nor keep talking and parading generalities. Definite words are definite acid tests.

Chapter XII

AN OBJECTION FROM SHAKESPEARE

WE have been insisting so much on the beauty of words and names that a Shakespearean couplet, that everybody has at hand, is sure to be hurled at our heads, and there is no dodging of it :—

> What's in a name ? that which we call a rose,
> By any other name would smell as sweet.

Shakespeare, no doubt, is a ponderous literary weapon to be thrown at a body. We must first see are we " kill't " —as an Irishman is expected to phrase it—before we pick ourselves up, pull ourselves together, and try to proceed.

Now it is quite probable that were we well read in this great English author we could give Act and Scene, chapter and verse, for lines that imply the direct opposite. Set a proverb to fight a proverb is tactful policy. Set Shakespeare to combat Shakespeare, a manoeuvre that equally promises success. In the one case as in the other, not seldom the accepted wisdom can be elided or the revered authority nullified or overturned.

No need, however, to go a-hunting or a-chasing over the ocean of Shakespeare for rebutting or ramming sentiments. It was not Shakespeare that set afloat this opinion sailing gaily but threateningly against us. It was Juliet, a precocious young lady who would be just fourteen years old " come Lammas-Eve." Surely the king of dramatists would not play ducks and drakes with all the proprieties by having the well-born, love-sick young damoselle soliloquize like a Solomon or a Timon of Athens, or even for that matter as one that knows anything about this bread-and-butter world of ours. She said admirably what just suited her there and then, but her authority is not the weight of a peacock's feather. And it is hers, not Shakespeare's. The English language gives a sly rap to constancy in her senti-

AN OBJECTION FROM SHAKESPEARE 99

ments—unjustly we believe so far as she was concerned or was conscious of them—by deriving from her name the unamiable word, jilt.

Further, the occasion was quite interesting on which this pert Veronian lady, Miss Juliet Capulet, was thinking aloud as, having been packed off early to bed, she leaned out of her balconied top-storey window. She was quite prepared, and we can see no wonder in it, for better for worse to change her own name; and, strange to say, she was hoping and praying that her Romeo, her acquaintance of yesterday, would be equally ready to " doff " his—what they should be known by afterwards did not enter into her wise calculations at all. She declares emphatically to the stars in quivering and quavering tones, with a beautiful accent we are sure, and in excellent lady's logic we are certain, that " it's but the name that is my enemy," not by any means the blood of the Montagues which ran in his veins. She would no doubt have gone on and on and have given to the listening moon half-a-dozen equally solid reasons to justify her determination to have her Romeo at all costs, had not Romeo himself at last popped out of the garden shades and suddenly interrupted her charming flow of talk.

A name, anyway, at such eventful times in life is, we understand, the smallest of small considerations. Nevertheless our young friend, Muggins, tells us in confidence that this is not his experience. He has, he says, his own troubles about home. He can't get over them and must go far afield. Shakespeare, we believe, if speaking *in propria persona*, would pronounce Miss Juliet's statements moonshine and sincerely sympathise with our Mr. Muggins.

Chapter XIII

IRISH PLACE-NAMES DISFIGURED

SLIEVENAMON AND DROMAHAIR—LOOP HEAD—MUTTON ISLAND—THE TWELVE PINS—THE OVENS—SION HILL—LEIX—THE CALF ISLANDS—A ROYAL PROCLAMATION—MEANINGLESS JARGON—HIGHLAND NAMES—AN INDIGNANT CORRESPONDENT—BURIED LABOURS.

"The face of the country [Ireland] is a book, which, if it be deciphered correctly and read attentively, will unfold more than ever did the cuneiform inscriptions of Persia, or the hieroglyphics of Egypt. Not only are historical events, and the names of innumerable remarkable persons recorded, but the whole social life of our ancestors—their customs, their superstitions, their battles, their amusements, their religious fervour, and their crimes—are depicted in vivid and everlasting colours."—"Place-Names," by Joyce, p. 79.

WORDS as words are of importance, as we have been endeavouring to show. But comparatively speaking, we acknowledge, that importance is small. "Words," as Johnson tersely puts it, "are the daughters of earth, but things are the sons of heaven." It is what they remind one of that really matters. Sound and derivation weigh but as dust in the balance as against that. Myles, to take a simple instance, as a Christian name for an O'Reilly, Turlough for an O'Brien are fine names, because admirably suggestive. "It is," states a recent writer, "the effort to do something beyond the power of words that brings beauty into them. This," he adds, "is the very nature of the beauty of art, which distinguishes it from the beauty of nature; it is always produced by the effort to accomplish the impossible."[1]

Now very many of the original Gaelic place-names are really artistic gems, and do accomplish the impossible. What romantic legends of fairy palaces and fair-haired matrons are conjured up by, for instance, Slievenamon! At a Sidh or magic mound, which is still pointed out on its

---

[1] *The Times Literary Supplement*, July 11th, 1918. First page.

eastern shoulder, the Tuatha de Danann dames wove their spells round the Fianna. Hence its name. It signifies the mountain (Slieve=Sliabh) of the fair-haired women (or according to O'Donovan, of the women of Fevin). What laudation of the district and its glorious scenery is not contained in the little crystalised poem Dromahair (Druim-da-ethair=the hill-of-the-two-air-spirits)! They had all Ireland to pick and choose from, these spirits of the air, the little poem seems to say, but they made a particular spot— a spot of unsurpassed beauty—their home. And it is such a spot; a spot of tumbling mountains and silent fern-flecked glens, and foaming cascades, beside a lake of brightness (Lough Gill); a spot whose beauty afterwards so enchanted St. Patrick that it was only because he was a saint, and a saint of an iron will, that he tore himself away with an heroic wrench from its enthralment, and ceased thinking of it, if ever he really did, as his ecclesiastical capital of Ireland.[1]

Irish place-names are never haphazard. Their modern substitutes, when not faint or distorted echoes of the old sound, are apparently lumped up any way. So many consonants, and a scrap or two of vowel mortared in between them to keep them together, and, to use slang, " there you are." If there be a ready-made word, whose sound or sense somewhat resembles it, to set up for it even this trouble is not gone to. They are sometimes absurd and ridiculous; if not ridiculous, practically always at least as empty of meaning as discarded egg-shells; mere gibberish, having, in the sense in which we are now discussing the beauty of words, no beauty or charm whatever. At best dead walls.

Let us first give a few examples, of their absurdity.

Cuchullin's Leap in County Clare recorded a feat of the Chief of the Red Branch Knights of Ulster. It is now Loop Head. It might as well be Mutton Head, or Rantan Head (we have just "built" it by taking consonants and vowels) for any sense there is in it or story it tells. It is the most westerly point in Clare and juts far out into the Atlantic.

There happens, indeed, to be a Mutton Island off the coast of the same county. It is a few miles south of Spanish

---

[1] *V.* Healy's " Life of St. Patrick," *sub no ine.*

Point, a term which explains itself. But, not to speak of their appropriateness in meaning, how much more agreeable to the ear is not the island's alternative name, Inishkeeragh, or its ancient one, Inis-Fithi ? It is recorded that about the year 800,[1] one fearfully tempestuous night Mutton Island was severed, as a Clare peasant expressed it, into three halves. But this carving up of it has nothing whatever to do with its present vulgar appellation—and vulgar it is in a double sense. Had it, it would be more tolerable.

The Twelve Bens of Connemara are now the Twelve Pins. They have as much resemblance to pins as cabbage heads—'not comparing them.' In Irish they are often called Beanna-Beola, that is the Peaks of Beola, and Beola was a great man in his day, likely a Firbolg chieftain. At Toombeola south of Beanna-Beola he was buried, and there plain enough, as plain as a word can make it, was erected a tumulus to him.

The Ovens is a village a few miles south of Blarney in Co. Cork. The Thomond Irish *oovan* is in English *cave*. At the place there are remarkable caves. Unlike the noted underground passages at Killashee, County Kildare, they are natural ones, " large and long with many branches crossing each other." They resemble the famous Fermanagh limestone caves of both Bohey and the Marble Arches, but are of greater extent. They are said to run for miles and miles. Were they advertised—that is blazoned on the dead walls and blarneyed about, as is the Lake District in Westmoreland in England, or as is the Giant's Causeway in County Antrim at home with us (the greatest 'take-in,' by the way, the writer for one ever had)—tourists would be tripping one another running to see them. Nor would they be here disappointed. Instead of that, the fine caves of Cork have been converted into " ovens." And so the sleeping bats, undisturbed in their palaces of grandeur, are sleeping still.

Sheeawn (Irish spelling sidheán) means a fairy mount.

---

[1] For a learned discussion as to the date we would refer the reader to the *ournal R.S.A.I.*, Vol. VII. 5th Series, p. 274.

What visions of fay and fairy and midnight revels can it not call up, throwing the glamour of poetry round the most commonplace hill or headland! Yet in Tyrone, Wexford, and even in Kildare, Sheeawn has been transmogrified into Sion. What the mounds—they are there still—have got to do with Jerusalem is a mystical problem far beyond us. We leave it to the natives to solve and settle. They ought to know, if anybody does.

A name that sounds through Irish and Anglo-Irish chronicles, resounding through them, one might say, like the great voice of St. Fechin of Corca Bascinn,[1] is Leesh (spelt Laighis). It was the tribal name of the clan O'More and was also, as was customary, the title of their tribal lands, a large and rich territory in Queen's County. As usual it was not a *vox et praeterea nihil*. It connoted that the clan derived from Lewy Leeshagh, grandson of him who in the first century had been Chief of the Red Branch Knights of Ulster. It was, moreover, a memorial of how the O'Mores won their spurs, when they drove the invading Munster men from Ossory's plains. Leesh shed all its noble associations when it degenerated into Leix. Leix has something of the old sound certainly. But it is a Danish word, pure and simple, and means—a salmon.[2] Possibly the anglicisers said to themselves, " It is good enough for them. These haughty reminders and reminiscences contained in Leesh are better censored out. They will soon be forgotten. It is too impudent, as it is, these Leesh folk are, and there is no ease in governing people till they are properly humble."

Leix—the salmon—has disappeared now completely off maps (one case already referred to excepted), and it is no

---

[1] " And when the Pope spake to him, and inquired concerning his travels," says his old *Life*, " Fechin answered him in a voice so great and masterful that the Pope was fain to turn away his head, not being able to support the volume of it." Nearer our own days Marshal Ney had a similarly powerful voice. In battle, it is said, it could be heard above the salvoes of artillery.

[2] Cf. *Leix*lip, on the Liffey, a wholly Danish word. A story is told of O'Connell and the shortest speech ever made in a Law Court in which this word figures. The suit was about water rights at Lax Weir near Limerick. The solicitor against made a long and labored argument out of the word lax. " It never was and never could be a strict right as the very word demonstrably shows," he concluded.

O'Connell got up to reply. " Are you aware," he said, " that lax in Danish means salmon ? " and sat down. He won the case.

great loss. But it is remembered still. Leesh is not recalled in the O'More country once in a blue moon.
"Of two such lessons, why forget
The nobler and the manlier one ? "

The range of rocks off Kenmare is termed by the old Kerry peasants Teach-Dhoinn, *i.e.*, Donn's House. In times far back Donn, son of Milesius, and all his crew were drowned there; and there their bones rested. The terminology recalls, as far as brief words can, the incantations of the wonder-working Tuatha de Dananns, and the storms they raised against the invaders in the midst of which Donn and his ship-load of warriors went down. Donn's House has been anglicised handsomely and bucolically into the Bull and Cow and Calf! The rocky group are now renamed the Calf Islands!

Loop Head, the Twelve Pins, The Ovens, etc., as well as Ringsend, Toberbilly, Newrath, Bear Island, and scores upon scores of other place-designations are—and Joyce is our authority—robbed of all meaning. They are as tapestry wrong side out, or as pictures with their faces to the wall. What Johnson wrote of Goldsmith may with equal truth be said—but reversed—of the foreigner in Ireland : *Quidquid tetigit deornavit*, whatever he touched he mauled and soiled and slimed in his stupid mishandling.

Nor was it done haphazard. If so there might be some excuse. It fits in with the sad history of the well-calculated misrepresenting and calumniating of the civilisation, and of the deliberate wrecking by the English of the language that was refined and profound before their own existed. There is a statute of Charles II declaring that " His Majestie taking notice of the barbarous and uncouth names [of Irish places] which hath occasioned much damage to divers of his good subjects " orders " comelie and reasonable English names " to be invented.

There is something monumentally English in this statute.

As to the terms once full of life and beauty, now not downright absurdities but, from which all significance has been banished, leaving them dead jargon, they are to be seen at every turn. They are as numerous as the evicted homesteads, whose unsightly nettle-covered walls alone sadly point to what once they were, in lonely Royal Meath. Scotch or rather Scots Gaelic is a language close akin to our own. Both are branches of the Keltic. More accurately stated, Irish is real old Keltic, Scots Gaelic a transplanted variety. The way in which our cousins the Scots—the sturdy Highlanders especially—have loyally held fast to their Gaelic names and their Gaelic spelling ought to bring a blush to our cheeks. Glasgow is pure Keltic (=Cleshu) [1] In " The Lady of the Lake " no line, for its sound, more persistently haunts the memory than the refrain of the Boat Song :

> Rhoderigh Vich Alpine dhu, ho ! ieroe !

It has both the swing and the echo of a verse from an Irish bardic school, from an O'Daly or an O'Flynn or some other of those Keltic Shelleys or Wordsworths of ours who are, not mute and inglorious, but unknown and unappreciated nowadays save by the learned few. Nor can any lover of Scott forget the incident in " The Lord of the Isles " on the memorable morn of Bannockburn when the Abbot of *Inchaffray* [2] went along the Scottish ranks barefoot, and as they kneel

> Blesses them with lifted hands.

It is so all through Scott. No Irishman needs a commentary on his personal or topographical nomenclature. To Gaelic-speaking Scots, and there are considerably over half a million of them throughout the world at the present day,[3] they are of course as clear as crystal.

Drop its literature and similarly take a glance at a map of Scotland, a large scale one by preference. Such titles as Maol Cheann Dearg, Fuar Bheinn, Beinn Mhor at once arrest the eye. And they are but three from hundreds and hundreds. The Guide Books, unlike ours—when we have such at all—regularly give the Gaelic name, the English pronunciation, and the meaning.

---

[1] According to a letter writer in the *Times Literary Supplement* (Jan. 2, 1919) its correct pronunciation is, not Glăsko (or the commoner Glāsko) but, Glăzgo. It thus rightly approximates nearer to its original.
[2] *Cf.* chap. xiv., p. 113
[3] This is the cautious estimate of a well-known Scots Gaelic scholar (v. *Leader*, February 15th, 1919). The last Census, he says, shows 200,000 of them in Scotland itself, of whom 18,000 can speak nothing else.

But, [indignantly complains the *Leader's*[1] thoughtful contributor who draws attention to this], the way the "official" forms of our place-names are jumbled up, ... and, worse still, often without any regard for the correct grammatical form or correct pronunciation, is a disgrace, and the fault is ours for putting up with it. Such forms as Bally for Baile, Boy for Buidhe, More for Mhór, etc., are barbarous.

The people of each district, he suggests, should take the matter in hand themselves. [Let them use the old Irish designation themselves first of all, and nothing else. Then] if a stranger asks a place-name give him the correct Irish name. If he wants anything else he had better—go look for it.

We cordially concur. His advice, too, is excellent. As always, on ourselves, not on Frank or Teuton, on stranger or stranger governments, let us depend. The Gaelic League should be as authoritative for Irishmen as is the French Academy for Frenchmen. The intelligent old peasantry, misunderstood and misrepresented—run down as ignorant, because, forsooth, they don't interlard their expressions with Shakespeare, and as brainless because they are " simple and upright, fearing God and avoiding evil"[2]—are many of them in this, as in other matters, fine guides and splendid scholars. O'Donovan, O'Curry, and Petrie, in their day did their best. But, no sooner was it recognised at headquarters whither their learning and enthusiasm were tending, than they were officially thwarted at every step. Their vast and meritorious labours were finally consigned to the dust of Royal Library lumber rooms. There they are lying still—if not moth-eaten by this. In his own neighbourhood everyone can " do his bit," and surely there is patriotism enough abroad to spur him on to the effort. He can help to blot out the sins and blunders of officials and verbal evictors, and to restore to honour the titles degraded sometimes by our unconscious countrymen following in the wake of the sneering, the too astute, or the bombastically erudite foreigner. Let us get back to what "His Majestie's" statute declares, grossly misdescribing, " the barbarous and uncouth names." They are both proof, the most obvious of proofs as well, of our ancient civilisation, and part and parcel of it.

---

[1] February 1st, 1919.
[2] "Singlemindedness," says Thucydides, "is an ingredient of noble natures." Long may it continue to be a characteristic of our Irish peasantry.

Chapter XIV
IRELAND AS A NATIONAL ART GALLERY

BATTLES — PORTRAITS — GROUPS — LEGENDS — SPORTS — HISTORICAL EVENTS—PENAL SCENES—LANDSCAPES.

"A painting has a right to be judged in the best light."—(*Art Critic.*)
"Never judge a picture by its defects."—(*Coleridge.*)

IN an Art Gallery are seen drawings and paintings of landscapes, battle-scenes, distinguished—or wealthy—individuals, incidents of affectionate home life, and so on; perhaps some pictures that aim at flattering solely by amusing.

They are, of course, of different shades of merit, some striking, some obscure. But a picture cannot achieve the impossible. The best of them leave a great deal to the imagination. A landscape, for instance, can present but one selected point of view or bring out prominently one remarkable feature of the scene. A battle can show but a single phase of the combat, one brief moment of a glorious or disastrous day. The Roll Call,[1] for example, was generally acclaimed the finest painting at the last Dublin Exhibition. Yet it represents but that; suggesting beautifully, though, a thousand things else.

Now, borrowing the ideas from the paragraph prefacing the last chapter but changing or amplifying the imagery, it is not too-far fetched to say that Ireland, looking at its place-names, is as one vast Art Gallery, hung all over with pictures of its decisive battles, its heroes and its saints, its ancient social customs, and even its sports and amusements. The indispensable Guide Book to that Gallery is Joyce's "Irish Place-Names," a book of poetry written in plain, matter-of-fact prose. It is not without some mistakes,

---

[1] By Lady Butler, a Catholic Irishwoman; wife, now widow, of the famous Irish soldier and author, Sir William Butler.

but it is more accurate by far than any Guide Book of them all. Of course time has dealt severely with some of these pictures; and barbarism, which did not either understand or appreciate, has much more seriously injured very many more. They are besides very, very old, most of them, and even painting two thousand or a thousand years ago was not what it is to-day. Then you are not to expect too much from them. They likewise can give but one incident of a battle, one prominent feature of a landscape or notable thing in a mountain or valley, in a hill or a dale, and leave the rest to the fancy. They make the effort to do something beyond the power of words, and that is what, as words, brings beauty into them.

Take then, please, the Guide Book in your hand. You have, of course, the map of Ireland hanging on the wall before you—that is if you are a person worth talking to at all. Now, sitting at your ease in your chair, with a stretch of the imagination and not a great one, you are in the midst of an Irish National Gallery; or even, anticipating the Ireland of, let us hope, the twenty-first century and the good times yet to come, you are in the centre, if you so will it, of a Provincial or of a County Collection.

In an Art Exhibition pictures are usually arranged any way. Size rather than subject determines the position. An expert visiting it can do very well without a Catalogue. After a general survey he makes for the best works and settles down to study them. Not so the ordinary individual.[1] For him a Catalogue is indispensable. Without it he is like a deer in a mist. By the ordinary Irish individual is meant in this instance a man knowing little about his country's history and less about its language. We are sorry to say the description is accurate; nay, if anything, flattering.

In a carefully compiled Catalogue, however, the paintings will be found grouped in some kind of order. Anyway, our ordinary individual will be first attracted by (A) Battle Scenes. Then he will wish to examine (B) Portraits of

---

[1] We stop short of saying "the man-in-the-street," though that is exactly the person we allude to. First, because the phrase is detestable slang of manifest English coinage. Secondly, because were an Irishman to use it of a sight-seer circulating round a picture gallery he would be put down as committing an Irish bull—and a cheap one. Though defensible it is not worth defence.

famous men, many of whom very likely figured in these combats. He is sure to discover that the features of some one of them are surprisingly like his own, and he will dally over it dreaming of the greatness a-coming his way, too, some day; for who knows? But he will leave it at last for (C) the Groups or Families. Next, especially if he is a young man, he will like to see depicted (D) the Legends and hear their stories. But he will hasten from them to observe (E) the Athletic Feats, in which again he may see himself as in a glass, if darkly. So he will dream his dreams once more; for do not, as Longfellow tells us,

> Lives of great men all remind us
> We can make our lives sublime,
> And, departing, leave behind us
> Footprints on the sands of time?

Should he happen, *mirabile dictu*, to have a taste for Irish history he will look out for scenes of (F) the Historical Events about which he has been last reading something; and will be pleased to obtain corroboration, quite independent of his books or documents, on the subject of the incredible barbarities of (G) the Penal Days. (H) Landscapes, of course, will be everywhere; if he has an eye at all for the beautiful he cannot pass some of them.

Let this then be the order we shall follow. Let us pick out under each of the eight headings half-a-dozen or so pictures. As there are hundreds of thousands in this vast National Gallery, necessarily not more than just a few can be specially pointed out. But that at least is required unless we go " awing " through it, and come away without any definite impressions.

A—Battles

You have then in the Gallery of Ireland sketches of " old, unhappy, far off things, and battles long ago." You have them by the score. That is just what is to be expected; the Kelts were ever a fighting race. With them *cath* means a battle.[1] Ard*cath* (Meath), Don*caha* (Kerry and Limerick),

---

[1] Embodied in a compound, even under any of its disguises, is not the term a better indication of the site of an engagement than the clumsy crossed swords which blotch our English-made maps?

and Derry*caw* (Armagh), we observe accordingly, are battle-scenes. Moreover, the pictures give each battle in its genuine setting. The examples we are standing before suggest one raging on heights (*Ard*-cath), another around a stronghold (*Don*-caha), and the third fought out in the gloomy shadows of the woods or forests (*Derry*-caw).

Furthermore, should one side have been utterly defeated (ruag=rout), as, for instance, happened at Ballyna*rooga* (Limerick) and at Maul*narouga* (Cork), that, too, is conveyed by the picture before you. Even the hideousness of a complete rout is brought out in such masterly touches as Lisnafulla (Limerick), the fort of the blood; Meenagorp (Tyrone), the mountain flat of corpses; Ballinamara (Kilkenny), the town of the dead; Glenanaar (Cork), the glen of slaughter, a name Canon Sheehan has immortalised. How helpless are the conventional symbols of the crossed swords on our maps to paint such vivid details of the surroundings and of the stricken field! In their own style of composition—a few, bold, firm lines, as it were, and no elaboration—no Roll Call can be acclaimed higher than some of these. In painting, however, as in poetry, comparisons are both odious and unfair. Every great work of art or genius is perfect in its own way.

B—Portraits

You have portraits of renowned persons—never of mere plutocrats, women or men—in Ardee, Armagh, Athy, Boyle, Benbulben, Bantry, Enniskillen, Glenosheen, Kerry, Larne, Rathcoole, Slievebloom, etc., etc. What a difference is there not? between calling a place in wooden fashion Rantan or Mutton Head, or even Cavan which simply means a hollow, and glorifying it by setting a gem or jewel in its name. Take Armagh, for example. It has embedded in it the miniature of Queen Macha of the golden hair. She founded Emania—whose remains one and a half miles west of the Cathedral town are still pointed out as Navan Fort— 300 years before the Christian era. Truly the poet writes:

> Ah! the little more—and how much it is!
> And the little less and what worlds away!

Ex uno disce omnes.

C—Groups

You have groups of individuals or tribes in, amongst hundreds of others, Coolavin (Sligo), Leyny (Sligo, and in Mayo Gallen), Corkaree (Westmeath), Calry (*passim*), Tyrone (=Tir-Owen), Inishowen (Donegal), and Tirconnel. They might be called great patriarchial familes. The MacMahons are very indistinct in Cremorne barony in their native Monaghan, and equally indistinct in Mourne, county Down, whither a band of them emigrated in the twelfth century. But they are there all the same. Allowance must be made for time and neglect. But the Cannons are plainly enough in Letter*k*enny. The O'Fogartys come out better still in Eliogarty, a barony in Tipperary; so do the O'Learys in Iveleary in Cork; while the great tribe of the Fir-Monagh (=the men of Monagh) that left Leinster and settled down by the shores of Lough Erne is clearly portrayed in the county name of their new territory, Fermanagh.

D—Legends

Beautiful legends are recalled, and each has one of its own, in Loughs Derg, Leane, Finn, Erne, Gillagancan (Donegal), Gowna (Cavan) Neigh, and Graney (Clare), in Loughandoul (Cavan) and the Loughnapiasts in many counties. Also in Abbeyfeale and Trevet, in Eskaheen and Coraglea, in Skeaghanore and Ballyconnell, in Tamlaght and Lisnagonnel, in Cloghaneely, where the Irish summer school flourishes, and in Knockcroghery, where they make the smoking pipes. As to these legends we can only refer you to your Guide Book. Space and time our excuse. Consult it, too, for the stories of the Fianna, epitomised in Lisnavena (Monaghan), Derrynafeana (Kerry), Cornafean (Cavan), Skeanaveane (Westmeath), etc., etc.

At an exhibition in London or Paris the legends, corresponding to these, adorning the walls in massive gilt frames would have some such titles as follow: Ulysses escapes Polyphemus; The Cyclops forge a Thunderbolt; Jupiter and Europa; Penelope's Suitors; Aphrodite Rises from the froth of the Sea; Saturn's Banquet (a gruesome affair in itself, but sublimated by genius and charmingly designed crockery); and a thousand and one other things, equally quaint and credible, far away and classical, and therefore beautiful, it must be. Our Irish legends are hidden gems.

E—Athletics

Sports and the prowess of athletes are pictured in the Urcher lot (urchur=the cast of a weapon). If the youths of Monaghan and Westmeath excel in hurling and in Gaelic football matches it is in no way surprising. Their fathers before them in the long ago were fleet of foot and strong in brawn and muscle. And there were champions amongst them, as the names Drum*urcher* in the one and Ard*nurcher* in the other testify. Cavan and Armagh also should be sporting counties. They, too, have their Urchers.

F—Historical Sketches

Dalriada (the extreme north of Antrim) has crumpled and crumpled and faded away. It is unrecognisable now in The Route which is seen in the same place. Though authorities like Ussher and O'Flaherty assert that it is a portion of the ancient appellation or picture, still it is doubtful. But it must be taken into account that this is one of the oldest of pictures. Over seventeen centuries ago the Scots copied it. They have taken better care of their copy. Scotia itself they carried away bodily from us, and Scots hold what they get.

Touaghty (Mayo) is still older than Dalriada. It is a picture of the Firbolgs drawn by the Milesians, and represents them as helots, or plebeians and vulgarians. But never trust a picture of the conquered by the conqueror, unless you are a fool. Antiquaries of the learned(?) Ledwich school call these subject races Attacotti. Pre-Christian Irish history has much to say about them.

That the Picts on their way to Scotland remained some time in Ireland is known also from history. It is considered to obtain support from the names Dun*crun* and Drum*croon*, both of which are in Derry, and from a Drum*croohen* in the parish of Devenish, Fermanagh. Cruith=colour and Picti =painted. In our Annals the country around Newry, Belfast and Carrickfergus, *i.e.*, ancient Dalaradia, is often termed the land of the Crutheni.

Donegal as a word is a representation of the fortress of

IRELAND A NATIONAL ART GALLERY 113

the foreigner. It might be translated or entitled a Gibraltar in Ireland. Fingall pictures their territory. Most probably these strangers were Danes. Wexford is certainly a pure Danish term. But on the whole map of Ireland there are not a score of names in all, out of its hundreds of thousands, that are Danish. This fact in the opinion of Joyce affords " a complete answer to the statement . . . . that the Danes conquered the country, and that their chiefs ruled over it as sovereigns." Incidentally we see the value of place-names.

On the other hand, in the middle and north of England as many as at least 1,373 names are Danish or Norwegian.

To deduce from both facts combined or contrasted the relative power and importance of England and Ireland before the eleventh century, no matter how they stand in the twentieth, is an easy corollary.

G—PENAL DAYS

Sad scenes of the Penal Days are before our eyes in the Affrin group, *i.e.*, wherever Affrin enters into the picture's denomination; sad but glorious scenes.

Affrin (older Irish aiffrend) is really the Latin word *offerenda*, as Mass is the Latin word *Missa*. This common origin tells its own tale, but it does not here concern us. Affrin literally means sacrifice, and is plainly ever so much a better term than the English one. The former with unerring instinct seizes on the very essence and heart of the rite; the latter concerns itself with the end of the ceremonies and a comparatively trivial little incident.[1] Affrin is embalmed in place-names *all over Ireland*; and from this fact, too, there are obvious deductions. Everybody knows many of these sacred spots. Our Guide Book describes about a dozen of them. All mentioned are either on high hills —as *Ard*anaffrin (Roscommon), *Cor*ranaffrin (Donegal), *Drum*anaffrin (Mayo), *Mull*anfrin (Cavan), *Knock*anaffrin (Waterford), one of the highest points of the Comeragh range (2,478 feet above the level of the sea)—or else in secluded dells and mountain gorges—as *Lugg*anaffrin (Galway), *Glen*affrin or *Glen*aniff (Leitrim). Never anywhere else.

---

[1] Viz.: The " Ita Missa Est," or signal for departure.

8

You can easily imagine you see the people assembled on a Sunday for the Holy Sacrifice on the summit of one of these high (Ard) or conical (Corr) hills, where surprise was impossible; perhaps sheltered from the winds and driving rain, as well as screened from observation, by the circular 'ditches' and hoary whitethorns of an old fort; as is half-said in *Lis*anaffrin (Kerry). Or else you can fancy them stealing in the early morning in ones and twos to the hidden glen, whence escape was easy and detection very difficult; nay, when nothing better was available, going down into a deep trench—*Clash*anaffrin (Cork)—to worship their God.

H—Landscapes

Such pictures are very numerous in our topography. For brevity sake it may be best to give the titles somewhat as the twentieth century—not the first or second century-artists would designate them, and as they might appear in a Dublin or London " Royal Academy Catalogue, 1920," and leave them at that.

Title of Picture	Present Name	Where Found
PLAINS—		
The Level Plain	The Moy	Tyrone, etc.
The Royal Plain	Maynooth (King Neat's Plain)	Kildare.
The Plain of the Flocks	Moynalty	Meath.
The Plain of the Allo	Mallow	Cork.
The Plain of the Dead	Moydow (But see p. 136)	Longford and Roscommon.
The Mountain Plateaus	Rehy	Clare.
Mountain and Plain	Claraghtlea	Cork.
The Open Country	Clara	King's County, etc.
The Honied Meadow	Clonmel	Tipperary, Dublin, and King's Co.
GLENS—		
Glen and Stream	Glanworth (The Watery Glen)	Cork.
The Mill in the Glen	Glenmullion	Antrim.
The Little Glen	Glentaul	Cork, Clare, etc.
The Windy Glen	Crumlin	Dublin, Leitrim, etc.
The Alder Glen	Glenfarne	Leitrim.

IRELAND A NATIONAL ART GALLERY

Title of Picture	Present Name	Where Found
MOUNTAINS—		
The Home of the Grouse	Lugnaquilla	Wicklow.
The Great Gap in the Mountains [1]	Barnesmore	Donegal.
The Little Gap	The Devil's Bit	Tipperary.
Summer and Winter, or The Snow-Capped Mtn.	Slievesnaght	Donegal.
The Mountain Church	Killevy	Armagh.
The Mountain Town	Ballintlea	*passim.*
The Weather Glass	Knockfierna (The hill of truth)	Limerick.
Proud of Itself	Benburb (Haughty Peak)	Tyrone.
A Saint's Retreat, or Royalty "far from the madding crowd"	Slieve Donard	Down.
WOODS—		
The Yew Wood	Youghal	Cork.
Bilberry Wood	Kilnafrehan	Waterford.
St. Finan's Oak Grove	Derrynane	Kerry.
Ravenswood	Brankill	Cavan.
Woodlands	Fenagh	Leitrim and *passim*.
	Fews	Armagh and Waterford.
	The Faes	Roscommon.
RIVERS—		
Marble Ford	Belleek	Fermanagh.
Opposing Elements	Burren (Rocky River)	Carlow.
The Church by the Bridge	Celbridge (Kildrought, Cilldroichid)	Kildare.
The River Mouth, or Child meets Parent [2]	Buncrana	Donegal.
The Dark Stream	Douglass	*Passim*, also in Scotland.
Land and Waters, or The Home of the Waters	Glashuna [3]	Cork, etc.

[1] Or possibly, Mountains do not meet. Friends may.
[2] Or, Arion meets Neptune, or etc., etc.
[3] —" A place abounding in little streams."

DYSERT DIARMADA

Title of Picture	Present Name	Where Found
RIVERS—con.		
The Abbey by the Stream	Abbeyshrule	Longford.
The Meeting of the Waters	Cumar	*Passim*.
WATERFALLS—		
The Salmon Leap	Leixlip (Danish)	Kildare.
The Fortress on the Cataract	Doonass	Clare.
The Plunging River	Owenass	Queen's County.
HILLS—		
The Long Ridge	Dromadda	Limerick, etc.
The Grey Ridge	Leitrim	*Passim*.
MISCELLANEOUS—		
Yew Tree Cliff	Altinure	Derry and Cavan.
Certain Promotion	Kilmore (A bigger church)	*Passim*.
Miscalculations, or perhaps War's Alarms	Templemoyle (The unfinished church)	Derry, Donegal, and Galway.
Do.	Kilmoyle	Antrim (5), Longford
Towers of Silence	Tory	Off Donegal.
Shiel's Monument	Carnteel	Tyrone.
The Carn of the Cats	Carnagat	Antrim and Tyrone.

There are, you observe, pictures without number, an *embarras de richesse*. A hurried glance is all we have taken of them. Fortresses alone, among the score of subjects passed by without even a glance, would contain a list longer than Homer's Catalogue of the Ships. No Art Gallery in Europe is richer. No drawings for their time are more deftly done and none could make a stronger appeal to an Irishman. One is tempted to delay for hours upon hours and read pages upon pages of the Guide Book, were it only

IRELAND A NATIONAL ART GALLERY

to show how justified is our simile or metaphor; or rather Joyce's. But then we fear to put too much before you. It would only confuse. We bear in mind an Enniskillen friend's story.

This Enniskillen man some years ago brought his youngest brother up to Dublin to consult a specialist. The little lad was about fourteen years of age, and the great Doctor's verdict was that his days were numbered. Naturally he wanted to give the poor fellow, who was not then very ill, a good time for the week before he went home to die. So he brought him up and down in the hotel lift; and he showed him the shops, and the ships at the North Wall, and Stephen's Green charming little park and the red-headed water-fowl and the black swan sailing about, and the Museums and Picture Galleries. Everybody was very nice to the manifest little invalid and he was delighted. The Dublin people are always that, God bless them!

The last day he brought him to the Zoological Gardens in Phoenix Park. They saw the elephants, and the seals dashing through the waters and plunging off the rocks, and the giraffes and the monkeys, and everything. Then the little fellow felt pretty tired and he sat down with him on a bench.

"Now, David," said he, "how honestly do you like it all?"

David, poor fellow, was very polite and was wishing to gratify his eldest brother, but he blurted out:

"Ah, John! my eyes are tired looking at everything. Everything is grand but I can't mind the half of them. One thing puts another out of my head. I would rather see a dancing bear in Enniskillen than the whole lot."

As the story's lesson is not quite lost on us we return to our definite town to examine how the principles enunciated in the previous chapter work out for it.

We are not a bit afraid, however, to assert that from our ten minutes' sight-seeing, with Joyce as our guide, we have brought away much more than the average tourist with his new and immaculate Baedeker or Murray in his hand, the red ribbon still dangling from it, carries away after ' doing ' the Louvre or the Luxembourg. Everybody that's anybody has been to them. Therefore he went. He can prattle now all his life—most indefinitely—about them and exclaim "grand," "magnificent," "superb," even "gorgeous" (if a confirmed poetry reader), and each of these in various intonations; and he will lug in references to the Louvre and the Luxembourg, garnished by these adjectives, on all possible and impossible occasions. That's about all of it. And that's what they call " culture."

Chapter XV

DYSERT-DIARMADA AS A PAINTING

RECALLS A GLORIOUS PAST—A KEY TO A GALLERY OF LOCAL PICTURES—A VERBAL SHRINE—ILLUSTRATION—THE SIN OF CASTLEDERMOT—CONCLUSION.

" It is a picture that must make its appeal as surely a thousand years hence as it does to-day." Said of Greuze's best picture.

ABOVE and beyond all, then, Dysert-Diarmada is to be put before Castledermot as a word-picture—in itself and for its associations and suggestiveness; for all it tries to say but, being but a word, it cannot. It presupposes our intelligence as every picture does.

Dysert, as we have already seen, is a word to cherish. But Dysert-Diarmada is a name to glory in. It brings us clean back, not half way, but all the way, a thousand years back, to the very origin of the town, and that a beautiful, may we say it? a blessed one. It is a full and vivid picture of that origin. The highest praise accorded the great French artist's masterpiece, *la Malédiction paternelle*, is the prophecy that it will appeal 1000 years hence as surely as it did on leaving the easel. So actually does not this picture? It links up the place with the golden age of faith, learning, and independence: when Ireland was the University of Europe, its " general mart of learning," as the English Camden says of it, " the school of the West, the quiet habitation of sanctity and literature," as the honest Englishman, Dr. Samuel Johnson, describes it;[1] and when it won its envied title of the Island of Saints and Scholars, which England has been making persistent at-

---

[1] Boswell's "Life of Johnson," *sub anno* 1777 (*V.* antea, p. 3). In the House of Commons on April 3rd, 1919, our present Scottish Chief Secretary paraphrased this. " Ireland," he is reported to have said, " was ' the Island of Saints and Scholars ' and did more for culture and religion and education in the early centuries than any other country in the world." The Belfast papers, as usual, either garbled this or excised it wholly from his speech. We have not seen the English ones

tempts to clutch from us; when, moreover, St. Diarmad's prayers and vigils brought down a blessing on the plains of Kildare, and his instruction and example enlightened and inspired Kildare's children. It connects it no less with a splendid past when Leinster Kings, who owed no fealty to Gall or foreigner, had their stately seats all over Hy-Murray, Moy Liffey, and Offaly or Hy-Failghe; and when royal Princes not only of Leinster but of all the four or rather the five provinces, nay often Kings themselves, were equally renowned either as proud rulers and chivalrous warriors; or—for then as always

" The best honours worn by man
Were those that virtue gave him,"—

they were illustrious, despite themselves, as lowly anchorites in their chosen solitudes.

A Castledermot, on the other hand, in County Kildare is a memorial of Kildare's downfall.[1] It is as much a symbol of sorrow, subjection, and humiliation, as is either the iron-caged laurel-crowned statue of William III on the old bridge of Boyle, or his horsey high-pedestaled one in College Green; or as is Nelson's uncouth 130 feet pillar which obstructs the principal street of Ireland's capital and which every fresh passer-by is compelled to look up at and ask, What in the world is it at all? These are attestations or emblems of the—alleged—conquest of this land of ours. They remind one of the ducal cap which Gessler stuck up in the market place of Altorf in the days of William Tell, and which every Swiss as he went by had to bend the knee to. All three, and there are many more of them, are —and little less is the name mentioned—pretty literally standing insults to the country. They were intended as nothing else. Placing them so carefully and comfortably out of harm's way, demonstrates with fair conclusiveness that those who put them up were perfectly well aware that they could not be regarded otherwise. Of course there are some men with dulled eyes who never think. There are more who want no bother or trouble. And there are all of us who wish more or less to obey the law, such as it is. But

---

[1] Cf. New Birmngham in Tipperary, Sydenham in Down, Bagenalstown in Carlow, etc., etc.; the street names of Dublin, etc., etc.

we know of no law, order, or proclamation, coercing and compelling a Kildare man to say Castledermot if he doesn't want to.

The poet prays :

> Sweet thoughts, bright dreams my comfort be!
> I have none else beside.
> Oh! throng around and be to me
> Home, country, fame, and bride!

We cannot, we are sorry, recall who he is who wrote those lines. But you can see for yourself he is a poet—nothing else.

Now, Dysert-Diarmada is a talisman to evoke such sweet thoughts and bright dreams from the shadowy, misty past. It is the golden key that opens the door to a gallery of such bright and beautiful local pictures. Castledermot, on the other hand, unlocks the entrance to a black charnel house, to a museum of sadness reminiscent of Madame Tussaud's Chamber of Horrors. Which of the two keys should a man of Kildare constantly carry about with him in his mind and memory? Drop the latter into a lake of oblivion deeper than the deepest pool in the Lerr or Barrow and have done with it. It is best there.

Castledillon, also in Kildare, and Castlekiernan in Meath, and many others "too numerous to mention," are objectionable on much the same grounds. No one would shed a tear if they met with the same fate. The Irish appellation of the former is Disert-illan, *i.e.*, St. Illan's hermitage, and of the latter Disert-Chiarain, *i.e.*, St. Ciaran's hermitage. The Gaelic names are as verbal shrines for these saints. The virtues of these friends of God may be as forgotten as the chivalry and the feats of arms of the Fianna, and their example and heroic spiritualism as ignored; but why act ourselves the Cromwell and batter at and destroy their shrines? Why try to cover up the honoured names as if we were now ashamed of them? Why anyway make a *bolahesh* or humbug of them? Illan and Ciaran and Diarmad are names that consort badly with palaces. Those distinguished by them lived not in embrasured, mahogany-furnished mansions but in lowly dwellings. No castles for them! Theirs a mission of simplicity, not of luxury; a message of peace, not of war, conquest, and plunder. Every household in Dysert-Diarmada should be as proud of the ancient title and as scrupulously careful of it as if they possessed one of the Old Masters. Kildare itself has not renaged its good name, why should its historic capital?

For there is far more than poetic sentiment or daydreaming, or balancing of sounds and significations, involved in the choice. There is a lesson and a good one, an inspiration and a clear and noble one. This we shall try to emphasise by an illustration, and conclude with it.

Among his Connacht friends the writer is happy to number a family called O'Rourke. Though now just peasants, they are, as may be traced, and as the writer took the minutest pains to trace, the lineal descendants of the chieftains of that name; as, no doubt, many of the Kildare peasant O'Tooles are descendants of the O'Toole of Hy-Murray, the Kildare Moores descendants of O'Moore of Dunmase in adjoining Queen's County, and the Kildare O'Ryans descendants, through Drona of Idrone in neighbouring Carlow, of Cahirmore himself who was monarch of Ireland in A.D. 120. Hence one should feel no surprise on meeting in an Irish cottage manners, courtesy, and unaffected simplicity that would be a rich adornment to a ducal palace.

In the hall of the present unpretentious home of the O'Rourkes there is a metal slab. It is let into the wall. The slab is plain but on it are roughly emblazoned the Arms of the O'Rourkes. It is in no way ornamental, yet for generations it is there.

"When I was a child," said the kindly, venerable old gentleman who showed it to me, " I was always askin' me father what it was. When I came to have sense he told me. My children in the same way used to be askin' me. I told them through time. My son's wee fellows be now always fiddlin' about it. Here's poor wee Owney here, God bless me wee man!" and as the child nestled by his side he patted the flaxen curls that were shyly trying to hide and bury themselves in his own long white locks, " Wee Owney here, he can make out, he says, the cat and a big bran. Bran is what we call our dog and he calls every dog a bran, so he does, and him not three till next All Souls' Day, if the Lord

spares him. Indeed wee Bryan—he's the eldest and a right manly wee chap he is." "Wee Bryan," he repeated when he had proudly told me his latest achievement, " he can say the rhyme off pat, every word of it, as well as he can say his prayers. It would do you good to hear him."
" What rhyme ? " I inquired.
" It's this," he said, " sure, I thought you knew it." I went down, I'm sorry to say, at once fifty per cent. in his estimation :—

> The lion rampant and the spotted cat,
> The hand and dagger comes next to that ;
> Those royal emblems doth well divine
> The O'Rourkes belong to a royal line.

He told me its history, too. The verses are not just Tennysonian, but they are all right.
"Wee Bryan," he resumed, " will not be long, please God, till he has sense for it, like another. Then the father will tell him. And he'll tell him, too, please the Lord," and he left down his little grandson, and, with his hand on the child's head, he stood up straight as a lance as he said this, " never to do nothing to disgrace the name he bears."
And so it goes on from generation to generation.

Now the people of Dysert-Diarmada are to be envied. In this, the true name of the town they were born in, they have a picture mosaiced from their best local history. It is a picture which speaks to them generation after generation, as distinctly as does the O'Rourke slab to the O'Rourkes ; and which, if they but attend to it, insures that they, too— to borrow our friend's beautiful Greek idiom of ' the double or emphatic negative ' [1]—shall " never do nothing " mean or cowardly, but shall always be good Catholics and good and noble Irishmen. Unpardonable to go and deface that picture. Monstrous to turn it into a caricature.
Alas ! up and down through Ireland the sin of Castle-

---

[1] We should like to add that the double negative, at which the semi-educated sometimes turn up their nose, is also true old Saxon idiom. It is now displaced by a piece of Latin syntax, and banished from " correct English " by the pedantic inaccuracy of grammarians. Three centuries ago it was universally used in England. It still holds its ground in the rural, less be-schoolmastered districts. Its presence in Ireland, in company with scores of Shakespearean survivals, points to the English Plantations.

dermot, the crime rather, is not unknown. This but an instance. Our ancient topography is in sound full-vowelled and beautiful, in meaning correct and most expressive. Pope Benedict XIV (in 1740) may remind us how "the Kingdom of Ireland" soon after St. Patrick's time "was called and really was the Island of Saints."[1] Pius V (in 1607) may show us how our ancestors at home merited the title, and Urban VIII (in 1642) testify that the title "was well deserved by a land whence came such hosts of saints to instruct other nations." But, besides papal documents and ancient chronicles we are not without collateral internal evidence to justify "the kingdom's" inalienable right to the envied designation. Our towns and counties, our valleys mountains and parishes, speak in tones equally clear; bearing, if listened to and understood, ample testimony to justify it. For our part we have been stupidly doing our best to stifle their voices.

---

[1] Lessons of the Office of the Feast of All the Saints of Ireland, November 6th. The Book of Leinster enumerates over 1,100 Irish Saints, 958 men and 150 women. The *Irish Messenger's* "Kalendar of Irish Saints" gives hundreds of additional ones whose names do not occur in the Book of Leinster. Pope Benedict XV, it is hoped, will soon add some hundreds more from more recent centuries to the golden list.

Chapter XVI

A READY-MADE HISTORY OF DYSERT-DIARMADA

LOCAL WRITERS—THE SACRED ISLE AND THE SACRED PRO-
MONTORY—CAMDEN'S MISTAKE—THE GAELIC LEAGUE—
HISTORYETTE OF CASTLEDERMOT—SUPPLEMENTARY FACTS

UP to this little or nothing has been given about the history of the town of Dysert-Diarmada except incidental scraps. However, it figures in so many events and has had, like its country, so many ups and downs, that double as many chapters more would, we fear, be needed to deal with it fairly. Outside of Dublin itself surely no place in Leinster can be more crowded with memories, civil and religious. We venture to assert that because, never anticipating that its mere name, as a sample name (apart from digressions), had so much to say for itself, we had been carefully searching out facts about itself. Local writers, however, could best treat of the subject. The late Dr. Comerford, the historian of Kildare and Leighlin, for one, in a contribution to the Kildare Archaeological Journal (Vol. I. p. 364) has already dealt with it fairly exhaustively. Other than local men would be as if walking on ice, and would need to step very cautiously. That their nervousness would not be very unreasonable, an example, akin to our previous discussions, may establish.

Carnsore Point in Wexford, whose *locus* is the extreme east and the extreme south of Ireland, where St. George's Channel meets the broad Atlantic, was known to the old natives as Carn.[1] The term explains itself. But Ptolemy, who flourished in the second century of our era, calls it the Sacred Promontory ('Ιερὸν Ἄκρον). Why sacred ?

---

[1] Ore is a Danish affix. In old Scandinavian it meant a sandy point.
—(Worsae, quoted by Joyce.

An American millionaire's home is, we are always told, a marble mansion. Accordingly the stoop is a marble stoop. To the noted Egyptian geographer just mentioned, his contemporaries and predecessors, Ireland was the Sacred Isle, *Insula Sacra Hibernorum*.[1] Accordingly this, its most important headland, was naturally the Sacred Promontory. For at least voyagers then making Ireland-wards, or setting sail Mediterranean-wards—to place the same answer in another light—it could scarcely be anything else but *the* Promontory of the Sacred Isle ; or, transferring the epithet of the too cumbersome expression, the Sacred Promontory.

This conjecture might satisfy well enough plain people. But it would scarcely pass with the well-informed. It is too simple. It displays no learning, no research into Phoenician,[2] Teutonic, or even Old Irish lore. The Englishman, Camden, is of the latter class. In solving the puzzle he states he has no doubt in his mind but that the preexisting Irish name had a signification like to sacred. (As against this we have just seen what it was—simply Carn.)

---

[1] So to the Latins. To the Greeks it was Ierna or Irin, and this is manifestly and admittedly, from their adjective ίερή (=hallowed or sacred). To a Greek, ancient or modern, the name *Ire*-land (a modification of this) would be no more obscure than is the Holy Land to an English speaker. *Insula Sacra*, if (as is most likely) a translation of the Greek appellation, affords the strongest possible corroboration of its significance. Festus Avienus both calls it this himself and testifies that " the men of old " (prisci) so called it. Dr. D'Alton in his admirably printed " History of Ireland " can hardly be made out to be doing full justice to the bare text of Festus by itself when he states (Vol. I. p. 4) that " among ancient writers Festus *alone* speaks of the Sacred Isle of the Hibernians." Half of the contents of the text is ignored. (For the full text, v. Lingard, I., p. 12.)

The Island of Saints, justified thoroughly in early Christian times, is apparently then a title of long descent. It is duplicated and not badly preserved or presented in the ordinary name of the country, Ireland.

[2] According to a writer who is something of an authority there are not more than fifty genuine Phoenician words extant altogether. Yet Vallancey, the learned, says he had compared a certain letter with twenty-six Phoenician Alphabets, including, of course, the Bobeloth one !

All Vallancey's lucubrations about Phoenician Ireland are based—so far as they have a basis—on an inscription on a stone on Tory Hill, Kilkenny. And he read the inscription upside down !

This stone weighs, as can be ascertained from its dimensions, about two tons. Another wiseacre of our own day, the late Colonel Wood-Martin, accounts for the reversion by saying that some young men, doing the running leap, used it as a ' spud ' !—(" Elder Faiths of Ireland," 1902, I., 160.) Kilkenny men are strong and athletic, everybody knows ; but they are not just Brobdingnagians. The Colonel's ambitious " Elder Faiths " is equally sensible throughout.

Knowing of the reversion of the boulder and of the true inscription (simply a stonemason's name badly done) Tighe's elaborate description of it is most amusing. Lever and Lover and Scott for all their imagination are thrown into the shade. (*V*. Statis. Survey of Kilkenny, 1802, p. 622 and p. 623, and don't forget the Plate, almost the length of the boulder itself.)

To support his opinion he avers that a place beside it, Bannow, bore the same meaning. Now Bannow the place, whether the island or the famous harbour where Fitzstephen landed, is twenty good miles west of Carnsore; and Bannow, the word, comes from nothing whatever sacred or blessed, but from something you may be inclined to call very profane—a sucking pig (bonnive)! Joyce is our authority. While anxious to do it, he failed to discover any nearer place whose signification by any stretch of imagination could be taken as resembling blessed.[1]

This Camden—we have just looked him up in a reliable French Dictionary (Larousse)—was a *savant*, in matters antiquarian and geographical, so wondrously learned that he was called the English Pausanias and the English Strabo. He was born and lived in London, too, with its consulting libraries and men and scholars, and died, unfortunately, in 1623. If a *savant* like him made such a blunder about localities he had never been to, what about people who can lay no claim to be either *savants* or astute and well-primed city folk; more particularly if, besides, they have never been south of the Midland Great Western Railway line? They would have need to look out, if they attempted to describe a Kildare town. It would cost them double trouble.

Anyway, when the Gaelic League supplements its splendid activities by seriously encouraging the study of local history, and be in a position to offer a prize, as we venture to suggest, for the history of the centre in which it is settled that their succeeding annual Ard Feis shall be held —as does the Welsh National Eisteddfod [2]—then gradually will our long neglected old towns, such as Dysert-Diarmada, wear at last their laurels, and the whole country discover itself and think more about itself. Too far east is west. *Virtus est medium vitiorum et utrinque reductum,*[3] writes Horace. It is not pride, but the lack of a little proper

---

[1] Carn may have had a previous or a duplicate name signifying sacred. But that would not rectify Camden's mistake about Bannow.
[2] It was held in Neath in August, 1918. On the 6th, the opening day, the prize of £100 for a history of the Vale of Neath was awarded to a Mr. Rhys Phillips.
[3] Virtue is the mean between two vices, and equally distant from either *i.e.*, it is the golden mean. *Omnis virtus in medio stat,* is axiomatic.

pride, that with us is the besetting sin. Windermere is a beautiful lake. It is beautiful mainly, we should rather say solely, because it is bordered by gentlemen's seats. Landscape gardening has done its best, and each seat is made the most of. Similarly, Ireland would wear quite a different aspect scenically if its naked hillsides were reclothed with their magnificent woods, historically if each county or each diocese had its sympathetically-written history. Any not too thin-skinned educated plodder can, for his own district, do the latter, provided only he expends money, time, and labour; and even landscape-gardening demands these three outlays. The Irish Walter Scott will yet come along, please God, who with his magic pen will throw a halo of poetry and romance around all of them.

Still, as both the reader may be disappointed, and as our indicated aim cannot be fully attained, if Dysert-Diarmada's principal interest be ignored, we feel bound to deal in some way with the subject. Now, Dr. Comerford's essay already referred to, "Castledermot, Its History and Antiquities," is too long, and is all so good that we would not have the heart to cut out any of it. But there is another printed article at our hand, ready-made, which, though far less scholarly and as sacking to silk in composition, exactly suits our purpose; or, as a merchant would say, fills the bill. It is, too, from a very old publication, the *Anthologia Hibernica*, which soon ceased to exist, as is usual with Irish Magazines that savour of learning, giving up in 1794, a hundred years before the *Kildare Archaeological Journal* first saw the light. Copies of the *Anthologia* are now rare. As to style and matter, it was the predecessor of the more valuable, if less pompously-named, periodicals, the *Irish Penny Magazine* (1833-34) and the *Irish Penny Journal* (1840-41). Both of these had a still shorter, but much more useful, career before they went the way of all Irish learned publications.

The article is found in the monthly number for October, 1793, and gets the place of honour. It is anonymous. But as almost all the facts up to the last paragraphs' are taken *verbatim et literatim* from Archdall's *Monasticon Hibernicum*, published in 1786, it seems probable enough that the author of this work is also the contributor to the Magazine. Possibly, indeed, it may be Dr. Ledwich, whose pen was busy for it, and that he boldly plagiarised from Archdall as in another glaring instance.[1] Whoever he be, the statements, as you see, either rest on or have the collateral authority of the Protestant clergyman last mentioned, a writer who for his day is trustworthy and very painstaking.

The *Anthologia* itself is, of course, malodorous with anti-Irishism and Liffey ascendancy perfumes. But then, what one is used to he never minds; and what student of Irish history is there who has not grown case-hardened, quite accustomed to these aromas? Exactly a hundred years ago Petrie observed that while historians of native origin were unable, owing to several circumstances which he adduces (none of which are to their discredit), to publish anything; there were others, of a different class and origin, who took up the subject of Irish history and antiquities in order to bring it into contempt; and, he avers, all but succeeded. They practically had then the field all to themselves, and it remains befouled with their prejudices.

We give the historyette of Dysert-Diarmada in full, exactly as it appears in this out-of-the-way Magazine. The "beautiful Engraving" is not reproduced. And it is a pity, for beautiful it is. The work indeed turned out by the Dublin publishers immediately before the Union can hardly be excelled. It is highly creditable to them. The printing both of Ledwich's and of Grose's "Antiquities of Ireland" as well as of this monthly, the *Anthologia*, is as good as could be desired; the illustrations for the time splendid. In Grose they are particularly fine, and the work is valuable if only for them.

---

[1] According to Weld, who, too, was of the [Royal] Dublin Society, Grose's *Antiquities*, edited by Ledwich (1791) "for the greater part has been merely transcribed." from the *Monasticon* of Archdall, published in 1786, a few years before. Grose, who did excellent work for England and Scotland, could have had little to do with this as he died a few months after landing in Ireland.—(Weld's "Statistical Survey of Roscommon, 1832, p. 225.) As to the ecclesiastical matter, this will be manifest to anyone who compares them.

AN ACCOUNT OF CASTLEDERMOT, COUNTY OF KILDARE:

With a beautiful Engraving.

Castledermot is situated in the barony of Kilkea and Moon, and though now only a village was a place of considerable strength, surrounded by a wall with four gates. The fabulous Legend informs us, St. Diermit about the year 500 founded a priory of regular Canons here, when it was named Disart Diarmuda; whence it received the appellation of Tristledermot, which it enjoyed for some ages, is not easy to conjecture.[1] In the ninth century [and also in 1040] it was plundered by the Danes; at which time there was a celebrated school here, in which was educated Cormac, bishop of Cashel, and who, on his decease in 907 or 908, was interred in this priory. In this age or the next, the round tower, old church and the crosses seem to have been erected, as they bear evident marks of belonging to these times.

Strongbow, earl of Pembroke, bestowed on the soldiers who followed him into Ireland, large possessions. To Walter de Riddlesford he gave the lands of Murthy and Imayle in which Castledermot stands, being the ancient patrimony of the O'Tohills or Tools. The third lord Offaley marrying the daughter and heir of Riddlesford became possessed of Castledermot and his other lands, and erected a castle in the town. In 1264, Richard de Rupella, Lord Justice of Ireland, together with Lord Theobald Butler, and Lord John Cogan, were taken prisoners by Maurice Fitz Gerald, and Maurice Fitz Maurice [of Castledermot], as was the red earl of Ulster. The Burks and Geraldines quarrelled about some land in Connaught, and filled the whole kingdom with war and tumult. A meeting was appointed at Castledermot, when the foregoing outrage was committed, and the prisoners sent to Fitz Gerald's castle of Ley.

In 1302, Thomas lord Offaly founded a monastery for conventual Franciscans in Castledermot, to which the family of Delahoide were great benefactors.

In 1315, Roger Mortimer opposed Bruce the Scottish invader: a battle was fought at Kells in Meath: Bruce was victorious, over-ran the country and took Castledermot, and the next year spoiled the town. Just before this, the Lord Justice made a great slaughter of the rebels at Tristledermot, who had risen against the government while deeply engaged with Bruce. The latter after destroying the Franciscan convent in Castledermot, and taking away the books, vestments and all the ornaments of the church with the most impious and sacrilegious violence, was intirely defeated by lord Edmund Botiller near the town. [In 1316 John, the eldest son of John, the

---

[1] *V.* however, antea, Chapter III. p. 13.

Earl of Kildare, died at Latreach Bryan, near Maynooth, and was interred in the Franciscan Friary here.]

In 1328, Thomas, the second earl of Kildare, died: he built St. Mary's chapel in the convent, and was interred in it, together with his wife Joan, daughter of Richard [de Burgh], earl of Ulster. In 1414, the Irish rebelled in Leinster; Thomas Crawley, Archbishop of Dublin, and Lord Justice, advanced as far as Castledermot with a small army to oppose them. He continued there with his clergy in prayer for their success; the event was answerable to their wishes, for the enemy were defeated with the loss of an hundred men at Kilkea.

A parliament [of the Pale] was held at Castledermot in 1499, on the 26th of August,[1] which granted to the [English] king [Henry VII] an impost of twelve pence per pound upon all merchandise imported to be sold, wine and oil excepted. Orders were also made that the nobility should ride on saddles, according to the English fashion, and should wear their robes in parliament, and both clergy and laity give the king a subsidy.

In 1532, Gerald, the ninth earl of Kildare, rebelled, and after destroying the county of Kilkenny with fire and sword, plundered the people of Castledermot, on a fair day, and killed many of them. During the rebellion of 1641, Castledermot was alternately in the hands of opposite parties; in 1650 it was taken by colonels Reynolds and Hewson. From that time its walls have mouldered to decay, so that now [1793] not a vestige remains. The castle and some parts of the monasteries still exist. It has six annual fairs but no market. The number of houses in 1793, was 163; sixty-three were of lime and stone and slated, the rest cabins. It has no manufactures, and is principally supported by the great post road running through it from Dublin to Cork. The round tower is still used as a belfry, no weak proof of its original designation.[2] The arch of this tower is semi-circular, and seems to have been adorned with the chevron moulding.

The *Monasticon* (1st ed. 1786) contains many more details. There are a few it would be a pity not to transcribe. We add them.

" Richard Keating, Gent." and " Sir Henry Harrington, Knt." were two of the " confiscators." To the former was granted in 1566 by Queen Elizabeth the Hospital of the

---

[1] A similar parliament had sat here in the reign of Edward IV.
[2] Lord W. Fitzgerald writing in 1891 in the *Kildare Arch. Journal*, states that the bell with its inscription is in the Round Tower still. We are sceptical about its being the original one though.

Crouched [1] Friars (part of the buildings was in existence in 1786, when Archdall wrote), and all the possessions it held for the support of the suffering and the needy—the endowments of the piety and generosity of the Geraldines and of the Kildare men. After that the poor and the old and the infirm of Kildare could—do as best they could. The " Gent.," we may be sure, never bothered himself much about them. To Sir Henry Harrington was granted in 1581, fifteen years later, the " Crouched Friars Priory " and " all its appurtenances." Knights in this country, from the Cootes to the " hungry Hamiltons," have had as capacious maws as the Cecils of England ; or almost as the Provost of Trinity, Hely Hutchinson. Of Hutchinson it was said " if he got all Ireland, he would want the Isle of Man as a cabbage garden." Plundering is the badge of all their tribe.

This Priory was located outside the town walls and adjoining the Dublin road. This 'great south' road ran through Athy from a very early period, but it was turned this direction about 200 years ago.

According to Archdall, Castledermot " was called anciently Diseart Diarmuda, and afterwards Tristledermot." He has no sneer about information received from a " fabulous Legend "—(v. the second sentence of the *Anthologia* article). The introduction of this whim is like the track of Ledwich's hatchet.

" St. Diermit's feast is celebrated on the 21st of June." The spelling of his name, by the way, is as capricious in Archdall as if it were old Hebrew and had neither vowels nor vowel points. He quotes faithfully from many records, and gives it, evidently, just as he finds it in each of them.

Among the many Abbots, of the institution founded by this Saint, whose deaths are mentioned, two or three are the most notable.

" The learned and pious Snedgus " was Abbot in the days when " Cormac M'Culienan, the celebrated Archbishop of Cashell, and King of Munster," was here a student. Cormac was slain in the year 907 or 908.

This King-Bishop was perhaps the most striking figure

---

[1] This term is an anglicisation, with a sneer embedded in it, of Cruciferi. They were Trinitarians.

A READY-MADE HISTORY

in both the literary and political history of those centuries. "He appears," says Hyde, "to have known Latin, Greek, Hebrew and Danish, and to have been one of the finest Old Gaelic scholars of his day, and withal an accomplished poet."[1] Of one of his extant books, "Cormac's Glossary," Dr. Healy writes: "There is no work in any living European language that gives such evident proof of high culture in the ninth century as this most interesting monument of Celtic learning."[2] A manuscript, copied by Duald Mac Firbis in 1643 from one still older, says of him that he was "a holy man, and the most learned of all who came or shall come of the men of Erin for ever."[3] Not very surprising that the author of "Ireland's Ancient Schools and Scholars" concludes his description of the "place of ancient fame, Disert-Diarmada, now called Castle-Dermott," by stating: "Its chief glory, however, will always be that it was there Cormac Mac Cullinan was educated, and there he was buried. It gave him knowledge, and when his brief and stormy reign was over, it gave him the rest of the grave."[4]

871 "Died St. Moylervayn, Abbot of Disert Dermot, and also of Killegie and Tihelly."

919 "Died the Abbot Carpreus, the son of Feradach, he was venerated and justly esteemed for his years and exemplary life; he was an holy anchorite, and, in his time, was at the head of all religion in Leinster."

May they all rest in peace.

FINIS

---

[1] "Literary History of Ireland," p. 420.
[2] "Ancient Schools and Scholars," p. 612.
[3] "Literary History of Ireland," p. 605.
[4] "Ancient Schools and Scholars," p. 425.

INDEX OF PLACE-NAMES EXPLAINED

In an extant ninth century poem it is told that Ilbrechtach, the harper, and the celebrated poet, Mac Liag, were travelling together over the Slieve Aughty mountains in south Galway. On Croghan Head they rested, and surveyed the prospect beneath them.

"Many a hill and lake and fastness is in this range," observed the poet, "it were a great topographical knowledge to know them all."

"If Mac Lonáin were here," replied the harper, "he could name them all, and give the origin of their names as well."

Mac Lonáin, according to the Four Masters, was "the Virgil of the Scottic [i.e. Irish] race, the chief ollamh of all the Gaels, the best poet that was in Ireland in his time." [1]

This incident goes to show the importance attached to place-names in remote times. The greater the poet the deeper his knowledge concerning them.

CONTRACTIONS USED

B., Barony.
C., County.
Ch., Church.
D., Diocese or Archdiocese.
d., District.
H., Hill.
Isl., Island.
L., Lake.
Mtn., Mountain.

n., Note.
P., Parish.
Pr., Promontory.
R., River.
Rt.W., Root word.
T., Town.
Tld., Townland.
V., Village.

---

[1] Hyde's *Literary History*, p. 427.

INDEX OF PLACE-NAMES EXPLAINED

A

ABBEYLEIX, V., P. (Kildare and Leighlin), Queen's County, 80.
ABBEYKNOCKMOY, P. (Tuam D.), v. Knock and Moy.
ABBEYSHRULE, V., Longford, 116.

AFFRIN, Rt.W., 113.
AGHABOE, P. (Ossory), Queen's County, n., 27.

ALTINURE, Tld., Cavan and Derry, 116.

Ard, Rt.W.=high.
ARDAGH, D., Longford and Leitrim, v. n. Kiltiernan.
ARDANAFFRIN, Tld., Roscommon, 113.
ARDBRACCAN, Old P., Old D., Meath, 22.
Ardcarne, P. (Elphin), Roscommon, v. Carn.
ARDCATH, Tld., P., Meath, 109, 110.
ARDMORE, Pr., V., P. (Waterford and L.), Waterford, v. More.
ARDNURCHER, Tld., Westmeath, 112.
ARDOILEN, Isl., Off Connemara, n. 47.
ARMAGH, P., D., T., C., 110.

Ath, Rt.W.=a ford, 80.
ATH, T., France, n. 80.

B

Baile,[1] Rt.W.=primarily, a place; then a T. or Tld., 106.

BALLINA, Vs. and Tlds. (c. 25), Passim, n.2, 30.
BALLINAMORE, T., Leitrim, v. More.
BALLINAMARA, Tld., Kilkenny, 110.
BALLINAFAD, V., Sligo, n. 2. 30, 116.
BALLINTLEA, V., Passim, 115.
BALLINTLIEVE, Down and Meath; Ballintleva, W. Connacht; Ballintlevy, Westmeath, variant forms of the same word.

Bally, Balli, Baley, Bali, and Bal especially on the east coast, are forms of Baile.
BALLYCASTLE, T., Mayo, v. Cashel.
BALLYCASTLE, T., Antrim—Castle.
BALLYMONEY, P. (Down D.), v. Muine.
BALLYMORE, P. (Meath D.), Westmeath, v. More.
BALLYMORE, P., Tlds., Vs., Passim.
BALLYNAKILL, P. (Clonfert D.), Roscommon, v. Kill.
BALLYNAKILL, P. (Tuam D.), Galway, v. Kill.
BALLYNAKILL, L., Galway.
BALLYNAMONA, Vs. and Tlds., Passim, v. Moing.
BALLYNAROOGA, Tld., Limerick, 110.
BALLYSHANNON, T., Donegal, 30.

BANNOW, Bay and Isl., Wexford, 127.
BANNOW, P. (Ferns D.), Wexford.
BARNESMORE, Gap, Donegal, 115.
BEANNA BEOLA, Mtn. Peaks, Connemara, 102.
BECTIVE, Old P. name, Meath, 22.

---

[1] The most prolific of all roots. Of townland names alone 6,400 have it as their first element. Pl. Bailte (pr. Balty) ; Dims. Baleen and Balteen. The last, frequent in Munster.

BELLEEK, T., Fermanagh, Armagh, 115.
BEN, Rt.W.=an eminence or peak. In Scotland, etc., a Mtn.
BENS OF CONNEMARA, Mtn. Peaks, 102.
Benburb, V., Tyrone, 115.
Bishop's Island, W. of Clare, 51.
BLA THEAGH, T. (I. Name), Kildare, 81.
BLACKLION, P., Meath, 22.
BOYHILL, Tld., Fermanagh, v. Coill.
BRANKIL, Tld., Cavan, 115.
BULL and Cow and CALF, Isls., Kerry, 104.
BUNCRANA, V., Donegal, 115.
BURREN, R., Carlow, 115.
BURREN, V. and B., Clare.

C

Caher (Irish Cathair), Rt.W.= a stone fort. Parent of more than 300 place-names. Over 30 Tlds. are exactly so called, and in several of these the original structures are still standing.—Joyce.
CAHIR, V. and P. (D. of Waterford and Lismore).
CAHIR, T., Limerick.

CALDRAGH, CALTRA, CALTRAGH, Rt. W., n. Kiltiernan.
CALDRAGH, Tlds., etc., Leitrim, etc.
CALTRA, V., Galway.
CALTRA, P. (Elphin), Roscommon.
CALTRAGH, Vs., Roscommon.

CALF ISLANDS, THE, Kerry, 104.

Carn, Rt.W.=a great pile of stones or mound of earth, 125.
CARNAGAT, Tld., Antrim, Tyrone, 116.
CARNSORE, Pr., Wexford, 125.
CARNTEEL, Tyrone, 116.

Cashel, Rt.W., sometimes translated Castle, 20. 50.
CASHEL, T., P., and D., Tipperary, 50.
CASHEL, Tld. and P. (Ardagh), Longford, Do.
CASHEL, Tlds., Cork, Donegal, Galway, etc., Do.
CASTLEDARGAN, Tld., etc., Sligo, v. CASHEL.
CASTLEDERMOT, T., P. (Dublin D.), Kildare, 77.
CASTLEDILLON, V., Kildare, 121.
CASTLEKIERNAN, V., Meath, 121.

Cath, Rt.W.=battle, 107.
CAVAN, T. and C., 110.
CAVETOWN, V., L., Roscommon, 15.
CELBRIDGE, V. and P. (Dublin), Kildare, 115.

Cil or **Cill**, n. 88.

Clara, CLARE, CLARAGH, I. Clar= a plain, Passim.
CLARAGHTLEA, Tld., Cork, 114.
CLARE ABBEY, P. (D. of Killaloe), Clare.
CLARINBRIDGE,[1] V., Galway, 22.

---

[1] The Galway shop-boys and *literati* declare this an ' elegant ' name. But it is a modern mushroom one, and a Castledermot one at that, and we are very glad to discover that it no longer usurps the place of old Kilcornan. For a Wesleyan ' district ' Clarinbridge would do right enough, and be quite appropriate. But for an 800 year old parish (or parishes), nay for a parish which before that, for the centuries intervening between St. Patrick's time, not very improbably may have been a little bishopric, there must be the gravest doubts as to its suitability or the stress of circumstances that would force it on them. According to the Registry of " Popish Clergy," in 1704 a Rev. John McKinine had his " Place of Abode " at " Killcornane." At Kilcornan, outside the demesne walls, the remains of his church are yet visible. Again at Kilcornan, quite close to the track of the Eiscir Riada, the famous ancient highway which from the

INDEX OF PLACE-NAMES 139

CLASHANAFFRIN, Tld., Cork, 114.
CLASHMORE, P. (Waterford and Lismore D.), 114.

Clon or **Cloon**, Rt.W., n. 22.
CLEENISH (now Arney [1]), P. (Clogher D.), Fermanagh, 22.
CLIFDEN—corruption of Clochan, V., Galway, 44.
CLONAGH, Old Abbey, Kildare, 16.
Clongall, Tld., Meath, 113.
CLONMEL, T., Tlds , Tipperary, etc., 114.
CLONMORE, Old Abbey, V., P (D. of Kildare and Leighlin), Carlow, v. More.
CLOONCLARE, P. (Kilmore), Leitrim, 21.

CLOONE, V. and P. (Ardagh D.), Leitrim, v. Clon.
CLOONACOOL, v. Coill.
CLOONEEN, Tlds., *Passim*, Dim. of Clon.
CLOONENAGH, Old Abbey, Queen's County. n. 2, 16.
CLOONOGHIL, P. (Achonry,) Sligo, 14.
CLOYNE, V. P., and D., Cork, 83.
COILL,[2] Rt. W.,=a wood.
COOLHILL, Tld., Kilkenny, v. last.

Corcach, *alias* Corcass=a marsh. 29.
CORCACH-MOR-MUMHAN (pr. Mooan) 31 and 86.
CORK, D., T., and C., 86.

---

second century onward cut across Ireland from Dublin to Maree, the ruins of a still older ante-Cromwellian structure are still to be seen—("History of Kilmacduagh," p. 415). On all our principles these facts establish a claim for Kilcornan. Away back in 1585, as an Elizabethan Record shows, the parish was distinctly "Kilcornan."—(Do., p. 239.)

Fr. McKinine, indeed, is put down as the "Popish Priest" of Stradbally. Stradbally, too, is an old parish name ; and, as can be inferred from the works just cited, was in existence a century before Fr. John was born. But in any case we would not be obliged to say that he preferred calling his parish (or parishes) after the village. For in the Registry there are many misprints, and even some names wholly wrong. The late Fr. Lavery, the historian of Down and Connor, carefully collated it with the original official lists still preserved in the Birmingham Tower, Dublin Castle, and he once informed the present writer of these mistakes.

Besides, we should like to add, there are many omissions. Not a few priests ignored the law and took their chance—of transportation. The subsequent Act of 1709 vindicates their foresight. It shows that, as they had suspected all along, the first enactment was just a trap. The later Act peremptorily ordered all the priests registered to take the Oath of Abjuration before the next new year's day (March 25th, 1710) under divers pains and penalties, jail and transportation being the least of them. To a man they all disobeyed the law and faced the consequences—(v. I.E.R., June, 1904.)

[1] Arney is run close by Shesha (I. *Seiseadh*—the sixth part) aged Cleenish coming in a bad third or an ' also ran.' In print, though, to all appearances Cleenish has as yet the field to itself.

The example illustrates the not infrequent mishap of the official parish title and the popular one being at loggerheads, a town especially being a dangerously disturbing factor. It is more than a pity if, as in the instance before us, the official one is so ancient that it goes back certainly to the sixth century, and most likely a long way further. Cleenish=Cluain Inis (see Index for these two terms), and of this local island-monastery St. Seynell was Abbot about the middle of the century mentioned. The substitution, either here or anywhere else, of the name of a common townland for a title having an antiquity that, if not already, will soon be "beyond the misty space of thrice five hundred years," is a crime as black in our estimation as any Enniskillen vandalism.

[2] Usually changed into Kill (and so confounded with Kill, a church) or Kyle. Also anglicised field, hill, and cool !

DYSERT DIARMADA

Cor,[1] Rt.W., oftenest a round hill, 113.
CORRANAFFRIN, Tld., Donegal, 113.
COVE, THE, T., Cork, 85.
CRANFIELD, Tld., Down, Antrim, etc., v. Coill.
CREMORNE, B., Monaghan, 111.
CRIT, CROTT and CRUT—representatives of Cruit, *Passim*, 29.
CROAGH PATRICK,[2] Mtn. Peak, Mayo, 27.
Crock,[3]=Knock anglicised, Ulster, v. Knock.
CROMWELL,[4] Tld., Limerick, v. Coill.
Cruit, Rt.W., 29.
CRUMLIN, Tld., P. (Dublin), Leitrim, Dublin, etc., 114.
CRUTHENI, land of, d., Down, etc., 112.
CUCHULLIN'S LEAP, Pr., Clare, 101.

CUMAR, Tld., *Passim*, 116.
Curragh—a morass. Also Curra or Curry, *Passim*.
CURRAGHMORE, Tld., etc., 29.
CURRY, V., P. (Achonry), *Passim*, Sligo, v. Curragh.

D

DALRIADA, d., Antrim, 112.
DALARADIA, d., Down and Antrim, 112.
DAMLIAGH, V., Duleek, 41.
DELVIN-NUADAT, Old d., Roscommon, n. 54.

Derry,[5] Rt.W.=an oak wood, *Passim*.
DERRY, P., D., T., and C.
DERRYCAW, Tld., Armagh, 110.

DERRYNANE, House, P. (Kerry), 115.

Desert Rt.W., *Passim*, 13.
DESERT CHUIMIN, P. (Cashel), Tipperary, 14.
DESERTEGNY, P. (Derry D.), Derry, 14.
DESERTMARTIN, T., P. (Derry D.), Derry.
DESERT-NUADA, P. (Elphin), Roscommon, 14.
DESERTOGHILL, Tld. and Half P. (Derry), Derry, 14.
DESERTSERGES, P. (Cork), Cork, 14.
DEVIL'S BIT, THE, Mtn. Gap, Tipperary, 115.
DISERT FULTERACH, Kildare, 16.
DISERT-CHIARAIN, Tld., Meath, 121.
DISERT-ILLAN, Tld., Kildare, 121.
DON or DOON=Dun.
DOONEEN, Tlds. (c. 30), Munster and Connacht v. Dun.
DONCAHA, Tld., Kerry, Limerick, 109.
DONEGAL, T., C., 113.
DOON, P (Cashel).
DONN'S HOUSE, Isl., Kerry, 104.
DOONASS, Half P. (Killaloe), etc., Clare, 116.
DOUGLAS, R. P. (Cork), *Passim*, 115.
DOWN, C. D., Tld., King's County, etc., v. Dun.
DOWNING and -INGS, Tlds., Cork, Carlow, Wicklow, etc., v. Dun.
DOWNPATRICK, T., Down, v. Dun.
DROM=Drum.
DROM, P. (Cashel), Tipperary.
DROMAHAIR, V., Leitrim, 101.
DROMADDA, Tld., Limerick, etc., 116.

---

[1] Begins more than 1,000 townland names.
[2] Previously Mount Egli, and perhaps once Slemish, St. Patrick's Slemish.
[3] About fifty townlands, almost all of them in Ulster, begin with this syllable.
[4] Anglicisation of Crom-Coill—sloping wood.
[5] Over 1,300 names have this as a prefix, sometimes a good deal disguised, and innumerable others have it as an affix. In most of them now you might as well search the Sahara Desert for an oak tree.

INDEX OF PLACE-NAMES 141

DROMARD, P. (Ardagh), Longford, v. Ard. Tlds. *Passim.*
DROMORE, D., Down.
Drum[1] (I. Druim, pr Drum), Rt. W.=a long ridge. Sometimes anglicised into Drim.
DRUMANAFFRIN, Tld., Mayo, 113.
DRUMCLIFF, P. (Elphin), Sligo, 79.
DRUMCROOHEN, Tld., Fermanagh. 112.
DRUMCROON, Tld., Derry, 112.
DRUMURCHER, Tld., Derry, 112.
DRUMURCHER, Tld., Monaghan, etc., 112.
DRUMRAT, P. (Achonry), Sligo,—rath.

DULEEK, B., V., P., Old D., Meath, 41.

Dun, Rt.W.=A great fort. Anglicised Down! Dim., Doneen, English Downing.
DUNCAHA, Tld., Kerry, Limerick, 109
DUNLEARY, T., Dublin, 85.
DUNMORE, P. (Tuam), Galway, *v* More.
DUNCRUN, Tld., Derry, 112.
DUNMOYLE, 116.
DUNDRUM, P. (Dublin); V. Armagh, Down, Dublin.
DUNMORE, P. (Tuam), Galway, *v.* More.
DYSART, P. (Killaloe), Clare, 13.
DYSARTAENUS, Old Ch., Queen's County, 14.
DYSART AENGUS, Limerick, 14.
DYSART and TISSARA, P. (Elphin), Roscommon, 15.
DYSART O'DEA, V., Clare, 14.
DYSERT-DIARMADA, T., Kildare, 77.

E

EASTERSNOW, P. (Elphin), Roscommon, 14.

ELIOGARTY, B., Tipperary, 111.
ENNISKILLEN, P. (Clogher), Fermanagh, 22.
ENNISKILLEN, T., Fermanagh, n. 1, 36.
ESTERSNOW. See Eastersnow.

F

FAES, THE, d., Roscommon, 115.
FASAGH, Rt.W., Kilkenny, etc., 29.
FENAGH, P. (Ardagh), Leitrim, etc., 115.
FEENAGH, P. (Limerick), Limerick, 115.
FERMANAGH, C., 111.
FEWS, THE, d., Waterford, etc., 115.
FEWS, THE, Bs., Armagh.
FINGALL, d., Dublin, 113.

G

GAL=Foreigner. See Donegal.
GALL, ST., T., etc., Switzerland, 56.
GALLEN, B., Mayo, 111.
GILL, L., Leitrim and Sligo, 101.
GLANWORTH, V., P. (Cloyne), Cork, 114.
Glash (I. *Glaise* or Glais=a streamlet.) Anglicised Glush, etc.
GLASHUNA, Tld., Cork, etc , 115.
GLASGOW, City, Scotland, 105.
GLEN OF THE DOWNS, Wicklow, *v.* Dun.
GLENANAAR, Tld., Cork, 110.
GLENANIFF, Tld., Leitrim, 113.

GLENFARNE, Tld., Leitrim, 114.
GLENMORE, Tld., P. (Ossory), *Passim, v.* More.
GLENMULLION, Tld., Antrim, 114.
GLENNADE, P. (Kilmore), Leitrim, 116.
GLENTAWL, Cork, Clare, etc., 114.
GOBAIN WOOD, France, 64.
GOUGANE BARRA, L., Cork, 86.

---

[1] This forms the first syllable of about 2,400 place-names, and is found incorporated in countless others.—Joyce.

H

Hibernorum, Insula Sacra, 126.

I

IDRONE, Bs., Carlow, 122.
ILLAUNS, Anglicisation of Oilean or Oilen, West Coast, 52.
INCH—anglicisation of Inis, 105.
INCHAFFRAY, Isl., Scotland, 105.
INCHBOFIN, Isl., Westmeath, 39.
INCHCLERAUN,[1] Isl., Longford, 38.
INCHMORE, Isl., Longford
Inse-, Prefix. Whence Inis-, Innis- and Inish-. Anglicised Inch-! 43.
INIS-FITHI, Isl., W. of Clare, 102.
INISHGLORA, Isl., W. of Mayo, 42. 52.
INISHOWEN, B. and Headland, Donegal, 111.
INISHKEA, Isl., Off Mayo, 42.
INISHKEERAGH, Isl., Off Clare, 102.
INISHMURRAY, Isl., Off Sligo, 42.
INNISFALLEN, Isl., Kerry, 39.

INSULA BOVIUM, Isl., Fermanagh, 38.
INSULA SACRA, 126.
IRELAND, n. 1, 126.
ISERT-KIERAN, Old P. (Cashel), Tipperary, n. Kiltiernan.
IVELEARY, P., Cork, 111.

K

KEELDRA, L., Leitrim=Caldragh.
KILBRIDE, P. (4 Ds.), n. Kiltiernan.
Kill, Kil, or **Cill,** Rt.W., n. 88.
KILL or KYLE, Rt.W., v. Coill.
KILL, P., *Passim.*
KILBEGS, Kildare, n, 12, 16.
KILBREW, Old P. (Meath D.), Meath, 22.

KILCOCK, V., P. (Kildare and L.), Kildare, 17.
KILCOLMAN, P. (Killaloe), King's County, 84.
KILCOLMAN, Ps. (Achonry, Kerry and Tuam), 84.
KILCOMMON, P. (Tuam), Galway, 78.
KILCRONIN, P (Kilfenora), Clare, 79.
KILCUMMIN, P. (Cashel), Tipperary, 14, 78.
KILCUMMIN, P. (Galway), Galway, 14, 78.
KILCUMIN, Ps. (Kerry), Kerry, 14, 78.
KILDARE, P., D., T., and C., 78.
KILDROUGHT, Old Name, Kildare, 115.
KILDYSART, V. and P. (Killaloe), v. Dysart.
KILKENNY, T. and C., n. 88.
KILLARD, P. (Killaloe), Clare, v. Ard.
KILLAUXAILE, Ch., Kildare, 16.
KILLEAVY, Ps. (Armagh), Armagh, 115.
KILMACDUAGH, D., Galway, n. Kiltiernan.
KILMORE, P. and D., Cavan, 116.
KILMORE,[2] Ps., Armagh, Down, Clogher, Dromore, Elphin, Ferns, and Killala, 116.
KILMORE, B., Cork, v. Coill.
KILMOYLE, Tlds.(5), Antrim, 116.
KILMOYLE, Tld., Longford, 116.
KILMOYLAN(?), P. (Tuam), 116.
KILLOSSY, Ch., Kildare, n.3, 16.
KILLPATRICK, P. (Old Name), Meath, 22.
KILNAFREHAN, Tld., Waterford, 115.
KILPATRICK, V., Cork, v. Kill.
KILTIERNAN,[3] Tld. (B. Dunkellin), Galway, Tiernan.

---

[1] Attempted thorough anglicisation—Quaker's Island.
[2] It is found in about eighty place-names, and at least in fourteen counties.
[3] Here are the ruins of a very ancient church, most probably one of St. Colman MacDuagh's (d. 632), Kilmacduagh. O'Donovan considers it probably the second oldest church in Ireland, St. Mel's at Ardagh, from which the Longford.

INDEX OF PLACE-NAMES 143

KILTUBRID, P. (Ardagh, D.) Leitrim,
n. Kiltiernan.

KINGSTOWN, T., Dublin, 85.
KINVARA, P. Kilmacduagh, D.),
Galway, 22.

Knock or **Cnoc**,[1] Rt.W.=a hill.

KNOCK, P. (Tuam), Mayo.
KNOCK, P. (Killaloe), Tipperary.
KNOCK, Vs., Clare, Down, and Galway.

KNOCKANAFFRIN, M., Waterford, 113.

---

diocese takes its name, being the very oldest.—(Ord. S. Letters in R.I.A.) The latter, Colgan states, was founded by St. Patrick himself in 454 ; and this, too, we may take as the date of the establishment of the diocese. Consequently it is probably the oldest diocese in Ireland. Kiltiernan is somewhat less dilapidated—absurd it would be to use the expression " better preserved," in regard to any of our old churches. Kilena near Kinvara in the same western diocese, and Kilrea in Tirawley near Killala are amongst the churches yet traceable as wrecks that rival Kiltiernan in age. All of them were stone structures of course, and the stones in massiveness are like dolmen roofs. So much the better for them. There is nothing else to save them and to stave off the day of total obliteration.

As to the first Christian temple ever erected in this country, as far as we can make out Kilkenny city seems to possess the strongest claims to the honour of having had it. It was built by Old St. Ciaran of Saighir (d. 465), styled both the Senior of the Saints of Erin and the Morning Star of Christianity, who is now the patron of the diocese of Ossory. It stood by St. Ciaran's Well, the famous Uaran. It is gone, of course. Even a chapel, that on the same spot succeeded and represented it, has disappeared, demolished in 1811 to make room for a " fish shambles," to borrow the unique phrase from the Corporation lease binding a Mr. Alcock to construct the " shambles." The well itself could scarcely be destroyed. It is enclosed now in the garden of the interesting fifteenth century structure in King Street.

But wherever the first and second, at Isert-Kieran beside the southeastern Tipperary hamlet of Mullinahone five miles from Callan, if tradition be of any use, was raised the third Christian church in Ireland. The place is now used as are Caldraghs (I. *Cealtragh*—a very old graveyard) in the north-west, that is for the interment of unbaptised children. Isert-Kieran for long gave its name to a parish, but it can be found now gracing no list. It is eclipsed, apparently, by a village title, or by the name of a fifth century Mummonian Waterloo. Can't well tell which. The sole place of worship, it is said, outside of Ossory dedicated to Old St. Ciaran of Saighir it deserved, one should think, more consideration and a better fate.

Relickmurry (=Mary's cemetery) also in Tipperary has equally fallen on evil days. Is it that the English propaganda—or the propaganda of English—was too much for it ? The cemetery, as is both usual and most appropriate, is the chapel-yard of an ancient St. Mary's. " Kilmurry," certifies Joyce, " is the name of nearly fifty townlands in which there must have been churches dedicated to the Blessed Virgin, for the Irish name is *Cill-Mhuire*, Mary's church." The fifty townland titles remain, it is presumed. But though Kilmurry crops up with fair frequency in the parish columns of the 1705 penal Registry except two in Killaloe and one in the diocese of Cork there are no parishes at the present time, outside of our cities, so distinguished. As to the lost Kilmurries it is better not to try to find out what names take their places. In contrast they must be low and mean, let them be what they will.

A Kilbride (the term needs no explanation) is still found in the dioceses of Dublin, Meath, Tuam, and Elphin ; a Kiltubrid in Ardagh, a Knockbride in Kilmore and a Knockbreda in Down and Connor. It would be a pleasure to be able to say that those fine old Irish Catholic names are never by any chance associated with others that you would think were imported direct from Kent or Devonshire by some new sect. But the pleasure is not ours.

[1] About 1,800 townland names have this as their initial syllable. Anglicised Crock.

KNOCKBREDA, P. (Belfast), Antrim, n. Kiltiernan.
KNOCKBRIDE, P. (D. of Kilmore,) Cavan, n. Kiltiernan.
KNOCKFIERNA, M., Limerick, 115.
KYLE and KNOCK, P. (Killaloe), Tipperary, v. Coill.

L

LAEGIS, d., Queen's County, 80, 103.
LAX WEIR, Clare, n. 2, 103.
LEESH, d., Queen's County, 103.
LEITRIM, V. and C. (P. D. of Clonfert), 116.
LEITRIM, Tlds., *Passim*, 116.
LEIX, d., Queen's County, 80.
LEIXLIP, V., Kildare, n. 103, 116.
LETTERKENNY, T., Donegal, 111.
LEYNY, B., Sligo, 111.
LIMERICK, D., T. and C., n. 32.

Lis,[1] Rt.W.,=the earthen rampart round a dwelling or fort.
LISDOWN, Tld., Armagh, v. Dun.
LISSANAFFRIN, Tld. and Fort, Kerry and Galway, 114.
LISMORE, P., D., Fort, T. and Castle, Waterford, n. 1, 29 ; n. 2, 62.
LISMOYLE, Tld., Leitrim, etc., v. Moyle.
LISNAFULLA, Tld., Limerick, 110.

LONGFIELD, Tld., *Passim*, v. Coill.

LOOP HEAD, Pr., Clare, 101.
LUGGANAFFRIN, Tld., Galway, 113.
LUGNAQUILLA, Mtn., Wicklow, 115.
LUIMINAGH, part of River, Limerick, 32.

M

Magh=a plain. Anglicised Ma, Mag, Maw, Mo, Muff, or anyway you like.
MALLOW, T. and P. (Cloyne), Cork, 114.
MAGHERA (I. *Machaire*), Rt.W.= Magh, Vs. and Tlds. (c. 200), *Passim*.
MAYNOOTH, T., P. (Dublin), Kildare, 114.
MAYO (yo=yew), C. etc.
MAULNAROUGA, Tld., Cork, 110.
MEENAGORP, Tld., Tyrone, 110.

Moing or **Muing**,[2] Rt.W., *Passim*, 29.
MOLLY, Tld., Fermanagh, Anglicisation of Malaighe—braes.
MONASTEREVIN, T. P., Kildare, 80.
MONEA, d., Fermanagh, n. 36, 29.
MOONE, V., P. (Dublin D.), Kildare 18.
MORE (Mhor), Rt.W=large or bigger, 106.
MOY (I. *Magh*), d., Tyrone, etc., 114.
MOYDOW,[3] B., P. (Ardagh), Longford, 114.
MOYDOW, Tld., Roscommon, 114.

---

[1] Initial syllable of about 1,400 place-names.
[2] I. Moin, pr. mone. Disguised as Mon, or as an affix—mona. Dim. Moneen.
[3] Joyce takes the last syllable as representing the Irish *dumha* (pr. dooa)— a sepulchral mound or tumulus, and the whole word to mean the plain of the mound. This is also Fr. McGivney's interpretation.
An equally probable opinion deduces the Longford name, *in toto*, from St. Modhain or Modan (fl. 591). During his life-time St. Modan here erected a Priory which, according to O'Donovan (Ord. Survey Letters), was the first of its kind in Ireland. No traces of it remain. The still older name of the parish, Kilmodhain, would lend support to this derivation.
From the 1705 "List of the Names of the Popish Parish Priests throughout the Several Counties of the Kingdom of Ireland," it is seen that a Fr. Patrick Ferrall in that year "pretended to be Popish Priest" of "Ardagh and Moydow." It is interesting to observe that of the same parish a namesake, the Ven. Archdeacon O'Farrell, is P.P. in this year of grace 1919.

INDEX OF PLACE-NAMES 145

MOYCARN, B., Roscommon, v. Carn.
MOYDRUM, Tld., Westmeath, v. Drum.
MOYGLASS, Tld., *Passim*, Glass=green.
MOYNALTY, P. and V., Meath, 114.
MOYVIEW, V., Sligo.
MUFF, (=Magh anglicised), Vs., Tlds., N. of Ireland.

Muine=a shrubbery, Rt.W. In 170 Tlds. Engl. translation Money!
MONEYGALL, V., King's County, *cf.* Donegal.
MONEYMORE, Tlds., *Passim*.

Mullach=a hill, Rt.W. In about 400 names. n. 1, 10.
MULLA and MULLAGH, MULTY and MULL, variant forms of Mullach. *Passim*.
MULLAGH, P. (Kilmore), Cavan, 60.
MULLAGHMAST or MULLAMAST, H., Kildare and Monaghan, n. 1, 10.
MULLAGHMORE, Tlds., etc., *Passim*, v. More.
MULLANAFFRIN, Tld., Cavan, 113.

MUNGARET, College, etc., Limerick 29, 30.
MUNGRET, P., Limerick, 29, 30.
MUTTON, Isl., W. of Clare, 101.

N

NAS=a fair or meeting place, Rt.W., Rare.
NAAS, Bs., T., P., Kildare, 9.
NASH=Nas, Tld., Wexford.

NAVAN FORT, Armagh, 110.

O

OGHILL, Half P. (Clonfert), Galway, 14.
ORE, An affix, n. 125.
OVENS, THE, V., P. (Cork), Cork, 102.

OWENASS, R., Queen's County, 116.

P

P. Few Irish names. *Cf.* n. 1, 62.
Piast=dragon or beast, Rt.W., Cavan, Derry, etc., 111.
PINS of Connemara Mts., Galway, 102.
PRESTON'S GATE, Athy, 83.

Q

QUAKER'S ISLAND—v. Inchcleraun.
QUEENSTOWN, T. P. (Cloyne), Cork, 85.

R

RAIBA, Old Name, Queen's County, 82.
RAMSAY, Isl., England, 32.
REHY, Hs., Clare, 114.
RELICKS, Tlds. (2), Westmeath, n. Kiltiernan.
RHEBAN, Ancient town, Queen's Co. 82.
RELICKMURRY, Old P., Tipperary, n. Kiltiernan.

Ros=a wood or a peninsula, etc., Rt.W., common, 78.
ROSCOMMON, P. (Elphin), T. and C., Old D., 78.
ROSCREA, P. (Killaloe), and T., Old D., Tipperary, 79.
ROSS, D., Cork, v. Ros.
ROSS, L., P. (Tuam), Galway, v. Ros.

ROUTE, THE, d., Antrim, 112.
RUAG, Rt.W., Monaghan, etc., 110.

S

SAN CATALDO, T., Italy, n. 2, 62.
SACRED PROMONTORY, THE, Wexford, 125.

SCOTIA, Old name for Ireland, Scotland, 112.
SEIRKIERAN (=Saighir-Kieran), P. (Cashel D.), King's County, n. Kiltiernan.
SHANNON, THE, R., 96.

SHEEAWN, v., Sidh, 102.
SIDH or SIDHEAN, Rt.W. Most frequent in Connacht, 102.
SIDHNE (pl.), English version Sheeny, Meath and Fermanagh.
SIDHNE, English version Shanes, Antrim.
SIDE-NECHTAIN, H., Kildare, 10.
SEEFIN, Mts., Waterford, 10, 11.
SION, V., Tld., etc., Dublin, etc., 103.

Skellig (I. Sceilig), Rt.W.=rock, Tyrone, Wicklow, etc.
SKELLIG MICHAEL, Isl., S.W. of Kerry, 43.
SKELLIG ROCKS, THE, Isl., S.W. of Kerry, 43.

Skerries (I. sceire), Rt.W.=Searocks, 18, 52.
SKERRIES, T., P. (Dublin), Antrim, Kildare, 52.
SKERRY, P. (Down), Antrim, 52.

Slieve, Rt.W =Mtn. Everywhere, 101.
SLIEVEDONARD, Mtn. Peak, Down, 28.
SLIEVENAMON, Mtn. Peak, Tipperary, 100.
SLIEVESNAGHT, Mtn. Peak, Donegal, 115.

SLIGO, T. and C., 30.
SPANISH POINT, Pr., Clare, 102.
STRADBALLY, Old P. (Kilmacduagh D.), n. Clarinbridge.
ST. FINBARR'S, P. (Cork), Cork, 86.
ST. CANICE'S, P. (Ossory), Kilkenny, n. 88.

ST. MULLINS, V. Bs., P. (Kildare and L.), Carlow, n. 2, 17.

T

TEMPLEMOYLE, Tld., Derry, etc., 116.
TEMPLEMORE, P. (Achonry), Mayo, v. More.
TEMPLEMORE, Ps., (Cashel and Derry), Tipperary, etc., v. More.
TIMOLIN, V., Kildare, n. 2, 17.

Tir, Rt.W.=territory.
TIRCONNELL, Old name, Donegal, 111.
TIRS-NUADHA, Old Name, P., Roscommon, 13 and 14.

Tobber, Rt.W.=a well.
TOBBERNOOAN, Roscommon, 15.

TOOMBEOLA, Tld., Galway, 102.
TORY, Isl., N. of Donegal, 116.
TOUAGHTY, Tld., Mayo, 112.
TRISTLEDERMOT, T., Kildare, 13, 130.
TUBBER, P. (Meath), Westmeath, v. Tobber.
TULLACHFOBHAIR, Abbey site, Kildare, 16.
TYRONE, C., 111.
TWELVE PINS, THE, Peaks, Galway, 102.

U, W, Y

UAMA, L., Roscommon, 15.
URCHER, Rt.W., Fairly frequent, 112.
ULIDIA, a sub-kingdom of Ulster on the north-east, Antrim and Down.

WEXFORD, T., C., P. (Ferns), 113.

YOUGHAL, T., P. (Cloyne), Cork, 115.

GENERAL INDEX

A

Abbeyleix, unique, 80.
Abbeys confiscated, number of, 6.
Aedh of Athy, his bravery, 81.
Aengus, the Culdee, 14.
Affrin and Missa compared, 113.
Aghaboe, an episcopal seat, n. 27.
Ambitions differ, 91.
American Atlas, a gorgeous, 4.
Amusing description, an, n. 2, 126.
Anglican Monks, the Caldey, 37.
Anglicisation of names stupidly done, 101.
Anglo-Norman Invasion, claims for, 40.
Anglo-Norman generosity, 81.
Anthologia Hibernica, character of, 128, 129.
Antiquarians, Old, as authorities, 39, 40.
—— R. S. of, visit to the Skelligs, 44.
—— paradise of, 44.
Apples, Devenish, 37.
Aran, St. Columbkille's Farewell to, 42.
Aran Visit, an, 48.
Archaeological Society, Kildare, 17.
Ardoilen, an Old World Museum, 49.
Assizes in Athy, made sure of, 82.
Athletes of Christ, the, 48.
Athy, origin and history of, 81.
Attacotti, what they were, 112.
Aubrey de Vere on Mungaret, 33.
Auxil, St. Patrick's nephew, 16.

B

Banagher, High Cross of, n. 19.
Baring-Gould's Lives of the Saints, 31.
Barry St., *v.* Finbarr.

Battle-fields, recent, with Irish names, 64.
Bell of Ardmore, loud-sounding, 44.
Bell of Inchcleraun, n. 1, 39.
Beauty of Art, essence of.
Benedictines, parent Order of all Orders, 87.
—— of Caldey, 46.
—— of Croyland, n. 1, 32.
—— Fort Augustus, 87.
—— of Glastonbury, 56.
Berkeley, Bishop, 84.
Bigger, Mr., M.R.I.A., his castle, 48.
Bishop's Island, description of, 57.
Boroughs and Cities, how they differ, 83.
Bravery of Irish Chiefs, 81.
Brendan, St., evangelises Iceland, 64.
Brigid, St., founds Kildare, 78.
—— legend of, 18.
—— her lamp extinguished, 65.
—— her oak, age of, 78.
Butler's, Lady, "Roll Call," 107.

C

Caldey Island, described, 46.
Camden, on the Irish Saints in Cornwall, 56.
—— who he was, 127.
Carman, the fair of, 8.
Carpet Slippers, antipathies of, 91.
Carpreus, Abbot, 133.
Carthage, St., 62.
Cashels, what they were, 20, 50.
Castles, Kildare, 3.
Castledermot, *v.* Dysert-Diarmada.
Cathedrals appropriated, 5.
Cathedral of Cloyne, 84.
Caves, famous, 102.
Churches, oldest in Ireland, n., Kiltiernan.

Churches, first built in Ireland, n., Kiltiernan.
Charles II's Statute, 104.
Chicago Degrees, 40.
Ciaran St., 62.
—— of Saighir, n., Kiltiernan.
Circular structures, vogue of, 50.
City, what constitutes a, 83.
Clans of Kildare, 2.
Cloyne, Origin of, 83.
Clogher's, Bishop of, rights in Devenish, 37.
Cobbet, on the Reformation, n. 1, 38.
Columbanus, St., 5, 64.
Colman, St., Mac Lenin, 84.
Comerford's Article on Castledermot, 128.
Comon, St., 78.
Confiscated Churches and Round Towers, 85.
Corcach Mor, Cork, 86.
Cormac's Glossary, 133.
Cormac MacCulienan, 84, 132.
Cornish Towns' Names, 56.
Courtmacsherry carpenter, the, 6.
Croagh Patrick, dysert, 27.
Cronan, St., 79.
Crosses, High, unappreciated, n. 18.
Crouched Friars, meaning of, n. 132.
Croyland, history of, 33.
Crozier, St. Patrick's, fate of, 65.
Curragh of the Races, 11.

D

D'Alton, Father, his reading of Festus Avienus, n. 1, 126.
—— considers it probable the, Nemedians, etc., are myths 16.
Damliaghs, what they were, 41.
Damliagh, St. Cronan's, cared for n. 1, 79.
Danes, did they conquer Ireland ? 113.
Danish place-names, number of, 113.
—— School of Antiquaries, 39.

Deoc an Doruis, the, 74.
Despoilers' ill luck, 7, n. 2, p. 10, 130.
Devenish, its foundation, etc., 34.
Diarmad, St., who he was, 77.
Donart, St., who he was, 28.
Drumcliff Monastery, 79.
Dyserts, Mountain, 27.
—— Fen, 29.
—— Lake, 33.
—— Ocean, 42.
Dysert-Diarmada, history of, 77, 130.
—— scores on sound, 89.
—— scores on derivation, 91.
—— wins as a place-name, 95.
—— excels as a picture, 119.
Duleek, its origin, 41.
Dun Ailenn, 11.
Dunlung, King of Leinster, 9.
Earl of Kildare, his generosity, 131.
Ecclesiastical Museum needed, n. 2, 36.
English, a mongrel language, 93.
—— the, what they have done for Ireland, 5.
Enniskillen, when founded, n. 36.
—— P. church, how flagged, 35.
—— vandalism, 35.

F

Fasagh Luiminagh described, 29, 31.
Father Pat, the great, his innovations, 22.
Fechin, Saint, 16.
—— of Bishop's Island, 52.
—— of Ardoilen, n. 2, 52.
—— of Ross, n. 2, 52.
Fens, Kingsley's description of, 31.
Finn and the Fianna, 11.
Finbarr, St., founds Cork, 86.
Finnian, St., n. 2, 61.
Fintan, St., of Clonenagh, 16.
Foillen's fate, 9.
Font, Devenish, 86.
—— Clonard, 36.
Fort Augustus, a modern foundation, 87.

GENERAL INDEX

Forts, what they were, 39.
Fridolin, St., the Traveller, 62.
Frigedian, St., 61.
Fulterach, Bishop, 16.
Fursey, St., 64.
Fynen, St., of Clonagh, 16.

G

Gaelic League, as an authority, 106.
—— a suggestion to, 127.
Gaelic Literature, wealth of, Preface n., v.
Gall, St., 56, 64.
Gasquet, Cardinal, on Irish scholars, 56.
Germany taught by Irish, 64.
Giants' Causeway, The, as a 'Showplace,' 102.
Gougane Barra, abandoned by St. Finbarr, 86.
Grose's Antiquities, character of, 129.
Guthlac, St., enters Croyland, 32.

H

Healy, Archbishop, Dr. Morrisroe on, 18.
Hector of Troy, compared to the O'Briens, etc., 84.
Hedley, Bishop, his simplicity, 54.
Henri Estienne's advice, 95.
Henry VIII, his ukase, 6.
High Island, v. Ardoilen.
Highlanders, cherish their placenames, 105.
Hill of Allen, 11.
Hospitality of the old Monasteries, 8, 19.
Hospitals, Monasteries as, 79.
House of Molaise, description of, 35.
Hutchinson's cupidity, 132.
Hybrid Words, 91.

I

Inishscattery, height of its Round Tower, n. 4.

J

Jilt, derivation of the word, 98.
Johnson, Dr. Samuel on ancient Ireland, 3.
—— on Iona, 45.
—— on words, 101.

K

Kells church, curios in, n., 36.
Kermesse, the Continental, what it is, 57.
Kildare, its castles, 3.
—— its clans, 2.
—— its confiscated convents, 8.
—— its outlines, 3, 12.
—— its Round Towers, 3.
—— when erected, 2.
Kilkenny Athletes, prowess of, n. 2, 126.
Killian, St., where born, 60.
Kilrush Abbey, 20.
Kingsley, Rev. C., on Hermits' Fens, 31.
Knockaulin, great dun of, 10.

L

Laserian and Molaise, the same name, n. 1, 36.
Laurence O'Toole, where born, 77.
Lawless, Miss, on Bishop's Island, 52.
Leader's indignant contributor, 106.
Ledwich's Antiquities, 35.
Ledwich as an antiquary, 35, 39, 129.
Library, the Cottier's Reference, 4.
Lindisfarne, Irish monks evangelise England, 56.
Lie, the hardest to kill, 40.
Lismore, School of, n. 39.
—— destruction of, n. 62.
Litany, Brother Antony's, 76.
Local History, 17, 128.

M

Macpherson, Chief Secretary, on " The Island of Saints," n., 119.
" Man-of-Affairs " on the ideals of religious, 57.
Marsh, the Great, of Munster, 86.
Martamane, Ogham Stone, 19.
Master Masons, St. Patrick's, 40.
McGowan, Tom., of the phenomenal memory, 76.
McMurrogh, Dermod, his death, n. 2, 7.
MacKelly's, their stronghold, 2.
Molaise, St., account of, 34.
—— as a name, disfavoured, n. 1, 36.
—— pronunciation of, n. 1, 36.
Monahan, Dean, on Banagher High Cross, n. 19.
Monasterevin, origin of, 80.
Monasteries, causes of their growth, 79.
Monea, church of, 36.
Monks of Caldey, conversion of, 46.
Monoa, Molaise's mother, n. 1, 36.
—— her vision, 38.
Moone High Crosses, n. 18.
O'More, Rory, 10.
Mount St. Joseph, Roscrea, 80.
—— Melleray, beginnings of, 28.
Mountains' names permanent, 95.
Moylervayn, St., 133.
Mullaghmast, massacre of, 10.
Mungaret, ancient glories of, 33.
Musée Plantin, the, 48.
Museum, Ardoilen as a, 49.
Museums, old world, 48.

N

Naas, a Royal residence, 9.
Negative, the double, pedants' objection to, 123.
Necropolis, an Abbey's, 51.
Nelson's Pillar, what it imports, 120.

O

Oak, St. Brigid's, 78.
O'Byrne, Count, appreciates antiquities, n.1, 79.
Ocean Dyserts, list of, 42.
—— difficult to enter, 47.
O'Curry's labours gone for nought 106.
O'Doherty clan, glory of the, 81.
Ogham Stone, treatment of, 19.
Oldest house in Ireland, 35.
O'Mores, origin of the, 103.
Orchards, Devenish, 35.

P

P. The letter taboo to the old Kelt, n. 62.
Paradise, five hours', antiquaries', 44, 49.
Parish naming, 21.
Patrick, St., his crozier burnt, 65.
Peasants excellent guides, 30.
Peasants caricatured by ' snobs,' 106.
Penal Days, pictures of, 113.
Permanency of place-names, 95.
Phenomenal Memory, a, n. 1, 76.
Phoenician Ireland, n. 2, 126.
Piaran, St., 62.
Picts in Ireland, 112.
Pictures of St Patrick, most inartistic, 71.
Pictures of Irish Saints unprocurable, 71.
Pilfering, Scotch, 11.
Pompeii and Inishmurray contrasted, 49.
Popes on " The Island of Saints," 124.
Portraits in place-names, 110.
Power, relative of ancient Ireland and England, 113.
Punica fides, instance of, n. 62.

Q

Queenstown Cathedral, what it is like, 85.

GENERAL INDEX

Querrins Round Tower, destroyed, 17.

R

Reformation in Ireland, Cobbet on, n.1, 38.
—— does not spare Caldey, 46.
Relics brought to Devenish, 37.
Rheban, an ancient Irish city, 82.
—— Lord of, his generosity, 81.
Rioc, St., Patrick's Librarian, 39.
"Roll Call," The, a beautiful painting, 107.
Romuald, St., 62.
Round Tower, Devenish, 35.
Round Towers, Kildare's, 3.
—— destroyed, 16, n., 17, 36.
—— their date and use, 85.
—— and confiscated churches illmatched, 85.
—— height of, 3, n., 4.
Ruins, Monasteries in, 5.
—— value of even, 39.

S

Safe, Brother Antony's, 71.
Saints, forgotten Irish, 54.
—— names and appropriated churches, 85.
—— number of Irish, n., 124.
—— their character and ideals, 57.
Salmon, Mr. John, Belfast, on stone churches, 40.
Science, old antiquities as a, 40.
Scots Gaelic, akin to Irish, 105.
——number speaking it, 105.
Sedulius, St., 61.
—— Abbot of Kildare, 61.
Shiel, the name, 61.
Skellig Michael, ungetatable, 47.
Soldier, Irish, pathetic description of, n.2, 52.
Solons, Tudor, 82.
Sovereign's Court, Athy, 82.
Statute, a monumentally English one, 104.

Stokes, Miss, on Moone Cross, n. 18.
—— her legend of St. Brigid, 18.
Stone churches in pre-Norman days, 39.
Story of Foillen's Fate, 9.
—— the great Fr. Pat, 22.
—— mollified eggs, 25.
—— O'Connell, n. 103.
—— the O'Rorke slab, 122.
—— Fr. Walsh's schism, 58.
—— the Tipperary Jarvey, 5.
—— the invalid in Dublin, 117.
Strongbow's liberality, 77.

T

Tennyson's Avilion, 56.
Tory Hill, Kilkenny, famous boulder on, n. 2, 126.
Treacy, Fr., S.J., Stanzas, 61.
Trimble's History of Enniskillen, n. 36.
Trinity Well cared for, 79.
Tuam, High Cross of, n. 19.

U

United States, Irish missionary zeal in, 58.

V

Vallancey on Phoenician Ireland. n. 2, 126.
Valour of the O'Briens doubted, 84.
Virgil of Sacred Poetry, the, 61.
Virgil the Geometer, 62.
Voice, a wonderful, 103.

W

William III, his popular statues, 120.
Wood-Martin, Colonel, his blunder, n. 2, 126.
Word Fanciers and Dog Fanciers, 92.
Words needed and words not needed, 97.

www.ingramcontent.com/pod-product-compliance
Lightning Source LLC
Chambersburg PA
CBHW050820160426
43192CB00010B/1834